*Thanks For*
*The Memories*

*For the office of Dr. O'Hara*

# Thanks For The Memories

A Humorous Story of
Marriage, Horses, Travel, and
Unconditional Love, Spanning Sixty Years

by

Aline Coutu

*Aline Coutu*

**DORRANCE PUBLISHING CO., INC.**
**PITTSBURGH, PENNSYLVANIA 15222**

The events, people, and places herein are depicted to the best recollection of the author, who assumes complete and sole responsibility for the accuracy of this narrative.

ISBN: 978-0-8059-7393-8
Library of Congress Control Number: 2006928015

Printed in the United States of America

*First Printing*
For more information or to order additional books, please contact:
Dorrance Publishing Co., Inc.
701 Smithfield Street
Third Floor
Pittsburgh, Pennsylvania 15222
U.S.A.
1-800-788-7654
*www.dorrancebookstore.com*

Dedicated to my closest friend, my dearest companion
through years of excitement, sorrow, and joy,
my husband of fifty-six years,
Albert Coutu.

# Contents

✳ It all started at Al's funeral, October 15, 2005. The day was dreary and it had rained all week. Inside the church, Reverend Victoria Burdick, standing at the podium, looked regal in her white vestments. She addressed the congregation with a broad smile, chuckled, and brought her hand forward, waving it in a so-so manner, indicating that after witnessing and hearing of Al's life and his escapades, it was a matter of doubt if those Pearly Gates would open up for him.

A dear friend of son Jack's, and now ours, Nancy Shanahan, played a variety of pieces, some classical and some liturgical, while people greeted one another at the rear of the church, and then finally assumed their places in their selected pews.

The first minister to speak had been Reverend Susan Stiles, pastor at the Episcopal Church of the Holy Spirit in the small coastal village of Charlestown, Rhode Island. She had prepared a traditional ritual for his funeral with prayers, psalms, readings, etc. She was stopped in her tracks and told that Al was not a traditional churchgoer, and her ideas, though thoughtfully put together "were not Al," and as daughter Lisa said, "True...he went to church sporadically but went to whatever church was paying my mother to play!" So, dear and caring Reverend Stiles announced to the congregation that the following service would be as much a surprise to her as to them all. She'd acquiesced that Albert Coutu's funeral proceedings should match the man.

Here was a fellow who had no qualms about racing some old lady to the only parking space available, who'd all his life lived "on the edge" in a manner of speaking, whose back porch, years ago, was the envy of the neighborhood with a profusion of geranium baskets within a day or two following Memorial Day. There were many

1

cemeteries on his bread route, why let those flowers die there when they would receive love, watering, and care at home with him? Besides, what an impressive gift from the romantic, goateed Frenchman to his beloved! Tons of flowers! Peck's bad boy had never truly grown up. Daughter Lisa and I would have to reprimand him about his attitude in certain situations!

Al had tried his civic best to join the volunteer firemen. The scenic little village of Dublin, New Hampshire, boasts the highest topographic town in the state. After taking classes as part of his training, he was now behind the wheel of the eighteen-gear semi-fire truck going up Dublin's very steep hill, having one heck of a time getting any of the three shifts into gear. He came to a complete stop, and then, horrors! The truck started to go backwards, as did every other car lined up behind him! When he related this to me, I asked him, "So what did you do?" He said, "I quit the fire department and joined the ladies' auxiliary" so he could "help them make sandwiches for the guys when they come back from a fire."

The service began and my thoughts drifted to the events of Al's passing, leaving me stunned, in a nightmare. Our daughter Elisabeth (Lisa) had flown up to Connecticut from Florida immediately upon hearing that Dad had suddenly and unexpectedly died. She, I, and granddaughter, Victoria, wrapped our arms around each other at the Marriott Inn in Milford, Connecticut, where Al and I had been staying after his surgery, and cried, and cried, our arms and bodies linked, three generations brought together in love, with one central focus. Pepe was gone. My girls were my "rock," and I was a zombie.

Al had been recuperating well after his heart attack and open-heart surgery, and we'd been planning how we would continue our trip home, back to Fort Myers. I'd arranged for someone to drive our car from Connecticut to Florida and reserved a handicapped room on the sleeper train. A cleaning lady had been hired to prepare our home for his arrival, being certain to have clean, fresh sheets on the bed.

Now, within four or five minutes, lying on the Marriott couch in our room, Al had simply stopped breathing. He'd felt a "little dizzy" for a short while, and then he gasped, "I can't breathe, c...can't breathe." Quick, short breaths followed. I'd placed my hand over his heart, stared into his eyes, and said, "You're panicking, you're panicking, try to relax, try to relax." Two short breaths followed, and he stopped, and I said, "That's it! That's it! Good! Good!" His eyes, still looking into mine, slowly dimmed into watery gray, as his head rolled to the side. He was gone. I was surely in a nightmare. Please, please wake me up. When the 911 rescue team arrived, I was still saying, "Please, please, wake me up." I needed to face my horror. I *was* awake, and my love, my companion of fifty-six years, whom I'd adored since I was twelve years old, had left me! I was angry. *Al, this was not part of the deal...how could you leave me like this!* We'd agreed long ago that neither one of us could live without the other, and should one of us have a terminal illness, we would go into the car, block the exhaust, start the motor, and go together. This just wasn't part of the deal. He was dead. I knew he was dead, and yet I kept repeating, "This wasn't part of the deal...how could you?" Although for many nights following his death, I would pray that I would not awake in the morning, it didn't work, and here I was, seated with my family and so many friends, as people who loved Al too spoke about him.

My daughter Lisa, my strength through this crisis, and whose courage and ability to work through problems or hard times is characteristically very gentle, took charge, planning each step of what needed to be taken care of. First, as Al had wished, we needed "to arrange for Dad's cremation." Secondly, did I want to continue on to Florida, or return to Rhode Island where we'd spent the summer, following our son's Jack's death and funeral? We would take one step at a time.

Summer had been bittersweet. Beautiful and handsome Jack, with his large moustache and broad smile, had finally lost his four-year battle with a gliablastoma brain tumor, having had an initial prognosis of six to eight weeks. Imagine! His determination, optimism, and personal strength, empowered by an incomparable circle of friends, had gone on for nearly four years, playing competitive tennis, doing construction, and running his three miles each day along the beach. Now it was over, and Al and I stayed in Jack's small condo in Narragansett, to clear up his finances and sort things out. We felt Jack's warm presence around us almost constantly. Jack was so special, and my heart was broken with his loss. I took summer employment as a musician in this church, the Episcopal Church of the Holy Spirit, where at first, still being in shock over Jack, I was afraid that my fingers would not remember where to go, but they did. Each Sunday, playing with a minister and congregation who shared my grief, I crossed a threshold of acceptance of Jack's death, and thanked the Lord that we, our family, and Jack's friends had had a bonus of nearly four years in sharing Jack's unbelievable spirit and courage. We decided we would return to Rhode Island for Al's funeral.

This time, we were not all gathered here for Jack. *Come back, come back to where we are now.* Lisa, with son Mike's long-distance telephone inquiries from New Hampshire, found a suitable and inexpensive funeral home for the cremation. On the very first night of Al's passing, I had been contacted by the New England Organ Donor Association, and as Al would have wished, donated all tissue and bone to them. Here was a perfect specimen, a man of seventy-six, fit, quick, never having been sick or hospitalized except for the removal of his tonsils forty-five years prior. (At the time of this writing, over fifty burn or cancer patients, or patients needing bone grafts/replacement, have benefited from receiving parts of my husband. I wonder if some of his humor, persistence, and great laugh have in some way seeped into their bodies as well.)

Lisa, Victoria, and I, in consultation with sons Marc and Mike, decided on the course the funeral should take. What was important in Pepe's life? Surely, I, whom he adored, his children, whom he loved unconditionally, literature, food, and music. Therefore, there would be music, readings on food, love, and marriage, quotations from favorite books and on friendship, joys, and sorrows.

So now we are here. Our years together are physically over, but the bond we'd formed for fifty-six years was eternal, and we would eventually be together again.

*Concentrate, Aline, concentrate? What is going on around me right now? Readings on food by Milne and on love and marriage by Kahlil Gibran. Where have we been? Oh my! Where have we been?*

# I Can Go Wit-Cha

✳ How did it all begin, this rare, profound combination? My upbringing had been that of an only child, with a very strict mother, so I knew well where my perimeters lay. Al was the oldest of eight, and he and his two rambunctious little brothers were very familiar with being booted out of a neighbor's yard with the threat of, "Go home! Go play in your own yard! I'll tell your mother." They were always in mischief, running here and there, without guidance, sadly, having a mother who was often ill.

At our small grade school, the seventh- and eighth-graders shared one large room, eighth-graders to the rear and seventh-graders to the front, with one exception. Albert Coutu had been assigned the very first seat of the first row so the nuns could keep a closer eye on him. I, being rather small, and in the seventh grade, was in the seat directly in back of him.

The same doctor, Doctor Legris, had brought us both into this world. From the first, I simply adored Albert. He was everything I wasn't, daring, inquisitive, quick to grasp a concept, and exceptionally quick to get into trouble. I was twelve and he was thirteen, and just beginning to grow a slight moustache. With his French accent, where the letter "H" is always dropped, and "R's" are unheard of, he would turn around, gaze at me with those big brown eyes, and comment about what I was wearing, or leave little candies on my desk. One day, entering the coat closet, I was surprised to see him in there already and he said, "It's a good ting (sic) that you're not alone, because..." the sentence drifted off as I exited as quickly as I

5

could from the closet. Many, many years later, I asked what he would have done, and he laughed and said he hadn't the slightest idea what would come next. I had strict orders from my mother not to speak to "that boy!"

After eighth grade, Al was sent to Mount St. Charles Academy for boys, in hopes that this keen enthusiasm and curiosity could be contained a little better. When letters were sent to our school (I was then in eighth grade) that told how he'd been punished or hit (that was permissible back then), I was heartsick. At about thirteen or fourteen, I had a strong dream about Albert being ill, wrapped up in a blanket next to the little potbellied stove in our classroom, and I was taking care of him. It was certainly prophetic of what would take place sixty years later.

We go now from 1943 to 1949. I am driving my father's car in West Warwick, Rhode Island, waiting at the corner of Curson Street to move onto Main Street. From a short distance, I saw a large black car approaching and in the passenger seat, *Oh my God! Be still my heart*, it was Albert, and I thought he saw me. He raised his hand and actually waved at me! My heart exploded! As it turned out, he hadn't seen me. He was just tossing out some cherry pits.

Al's sister, Jeanne, was a good friend, and every Monday we would play tennis together. Soon after the cherry-pit incident, the phone rang and it was Albert. "My sista forgot her sweata in your car."

"I know," I replied, "I'll have it with me when I pick her up today."

"Well, Jeanne can't go wit-cha today, but *I* can go wit-cha."

What a line for a first date! Well, we played tennis and I beat him, a few times. Al gave up on tennis but found other ways of dating, football games, playing cards or shooting pool with my father, going to eat or to the movies. Sometimes we would go to his house, where he lived with his parents, and he would cook a meal for me.

The first kiss took place nowhere near the first date. It was very nervously approached with my back against the refrigerator door, in such a gentle manner well into our courtship. No great love scenes, but a sincere, caring bond between two people who loved each other deeply and looked ahead to a life together.

Back in Holy Spirit Church, Nancy, Maria Day, and Marianne Lombardi sang "Ubi Caritas." The text is: "Ubi caritas, et amor, ubi caritas Deus ibi est." The translation is: "Live in charity and steadfast love. Live in charity and God will dwell with you." *How fitting*, I thought.

Next to the three ladies, the largest arrangement of flowers I'd ever seen had been placed on the floor in front of the altar, and read, "With love, from the Harem." I'm sure that anyone noticing the card but not knowing the history of "the Harem," must have been quite impressed with Al's prowess, at seventy-six years of age, charming so many ladies now being referred to as "the Harem."

# *Lisa's Eulogy*

✳ Lisa began speaking, and in a strong, but occasionally quivering voice, read the eulogy she'd prepared for her father the night before. It went as follows:

"In all the time I was growing up I never saw my parents apart. They were so close I always considered them basically one and the same. I always referred to them collectively as 'Mom.' Although both of my parents always worked full time, when they were at home, my mom handled all the finances while my dad cooked and cleaned. Their lives were so intertwined, it is difficult to speak of one without the other.

"My parents created this bubble for me to grow up in. Looking back, I am always amazed at how far removed I was from subjects like divorce, alcoholism, abuse, or violence of any kind. I think the only notable vice which ran rampant throughout my adolescence was rather extreme impatient cursing by my father.

"Day by day, month by month, year by year, my parents gradually shed pollen-sized characteristics of themselves which I inevitably inhaled into the deepest part of my being. Sometimes, I wonder why I view the world in a certain way, and I always come back to the same place, 'Mom' plural." *I was amazed, listening to Lisa speak, by how inner-directed her comments were. Did Al and I actually spawn this amazing young woman standing there at the podium, with such incomprehensible perception?*

Lisa continued speaking. "Although extremely intelligent, curious, and introspective, my dad was not a complicated man. He

8

consciously and yet unconsciously had a very clear idea what his priorities were. First was his undying love for my mom and his willingness to please her. She was without question the most important part of his life. Second, although my father could be intolerant and impatient with people outside, he loved his family and accepted his children unconditionally, regardless of their transgressions. He always sought family cohesiveness.

"My dad had a strong work ethic. It was important to work hard and be dependable. My dad never left a job unfinished and performed even the most menial task to the best of his ability. He never *watched* others work, but always chipped in and lent a helping hand. Even if he didn't have a clue how to perform a particular task, he would give it a try despite the possible injuries that may ensue.

"Pearls of wisdom that have always stuck in my mind: 1. There is no free lunch. 2. Don't go empty-handed (clearing the table, emptying the car). 3. Why do it slow when you can do it fast?

"My dad was born in an era when certain topics were taboo. Men were the breadwinners, and women ran the household. My dad just didn't seem to notice. He did what needed to be done without complaint and without a care for what others thought. He was the nurturer, the glue. Shortly after we moved to Dublin, New Hampshire, my father decided to join the fire department. There were several tests he needed to pass in order to be a fireman. Try as he may, he was unable to drive the fire truck up the very steep hill which went up to the center of town. Undaunted by this setback, he simply joined the ladies' auxiliary.

"I was always impressed at how well my dad adjusted to new situations. Keeping up with my mom is no easy task. She was born with a bad case of wanderlust." *True. Knowing that Al would be very reticent to leave his home, his comfort zone, I simply would make the plans, purchase the flight tickets, and say to him, "I've got two tickets to fly to Paris. Do you want to come with me?"*

Lisa continued her eulogy: "Without notice my mom would decide to take a trip somewhere and unless he wanted to be left behind (which just wasn't an option) he had to pack up and get going." *Oh dear God! Lisa was very observant. Had she been reading my mind all these years? Did she know me better than I knew myself?*

Lisa went on. "In recent years, he'd developed his own 'flexi-plan' for team loyalty. He was constantly switching between football teams, depending on which team was winning. He'd say, 'You can't lose when you stick with the winners.'

"The quality I loved the best about my dad was his ability to laugh, to make others laugh, and to laugh at himself. He had a great laugh, and just hearing his laugh would make me laugh. I will admit, my father was not perfect. He would be extremely impatient and had quite a temper which inevitably would get him into trouble with others.

"Apparently, when my parents were first married, my mom made the mistake of beating my dad at a game of cards. He was not a good loser. He threw Mom's slippers out the window and then ripped up the cards" (*throwing the entire pack of cards up in the air, tearing them in pieces as they floated down*). "The slippers resided on the neighbors' roof for months after, but the laughter generated by the retelling of this story continues fifty years later.

"I could continue for quite some time about the virtues and exploits to my 'Mom' plural. The stories are truly endless. I thank all of you for sharing this time of reflection with me and our family. If there are any of you who would like to share your memories of Albert, please do so now."

One after the other, old family friends, and friends and classmates of Al's at the University of Rhode Island had come from near and far to tell Al how they'd felt about him. They related how Al had helped them when they needed help, and these grown men were sobbing as they left the podium. Lisa was right. Al never shirked at any job, and gave his all to the task at hand.

My mother did not like Al. She had greater aspirations as to who my life should be spent with. But this was a time when she was not well and very vulnerable. She resentfully said, "Go ahead, get married. It will never last!"

As a wedding gift, in October 1950, Al's parents offered us either a flight to Miami Beach or a refrigerator. Obviously, we chose the least practical, the flight to Miami Beach, which set a precedent for many future choices and situations to come. We were so naïve, first-time travelers, excluding visiting our relatives in Canada. We very nearly purchased a lace tablecloth, which had "taken seven nuns seven years" to make. Fortunately, Uncle Cleo, a burly, husky, intimidating semi-trailer truck driver, convinced the sellers of this fraud to return our money. We were babes in the woods.

Our first night before flying to Miami Beach was spent at the Commodore Hotel in New York City. Although Al at some later time confided that as a child he'd played "doctor" with certain boys and girls in his neighborhood, we were truly virgins. That traditionally frightening first night, especially for a convent girl, was experimental and truly funny! Poor Al, trying to establish his manhood, while the Commodore sign outside our window flashed red on and off into our room, highlighting his attributes, which had me giggling and laughing. I had never seen anything like that before. With the persistence that he was always known for, he was successful, and it was so comforting to have Al's beautiful strong body next to mine. I stopped laughing somewhere in there, and was just so happy that we were "one" and so much in love.

We returned to West Warwick where we established our home and he continued working at Al's Restaurant. He would be up at 4:00 A.M. day by day, without fail. If we were snowed in, he would trudge the mile to the restaurant to open up in time for the milkmen and tradesmen who depended on their breakfast at 5:00 A.M. One morning, while preparing his clam chowder in time for lunch, the chowder was boiling and he poured in the chopped onions; they did not separate, but fell into the chowder like a solid bomb. The boiling, greasy chowder splashed up on his hand, and he immediately wiped the back of his hand against his apron. The skin stayed on the apron and the top of his hand was nearly devoid of any skin at all. He wrapped his hand and continued working. Each morning, we would both get up at 3:00 A.M. and I had the task of changing his bandages. I would cry doing this, knowing the pain he was going through, and yet he was not complaining except for a few words, cursing himself for having let that happen. He worked every day through the weeks of pain while new skin grew.

Recently, our oldest son, Marc, related a little story that I'd never heard, in keeping with Al's philosophy of, "Why do it slow when you can do it fast?" Apparently, Al, Marc, and Jack were building and painting jumps for the hunt course. Al was trying to remove the cover which had become securely glued to the paint can. In attempting to punch holes into the cover, thereby letting air underneath it to make its removal easier, Al had been quickly, as usual, punching holes with the screw driver, and Marc came into the workshop observing that Al's hand was pinned to the cover with the screwdriver, with many expletives about the screwdriver and the can cover being emitted by Al. Embarrassed, Al saw Marc, pulled the screwdriver out, washed his hands, and after placing a Band-Aid over the wound, went right back to his project. Marc had to promise that he would not relate the incident to anyone in the family, "especially Mom."

# Children

The babies began coming. Marc in 1951, and then Jack in 1953. In 1955, the first little girl was born. She lived one day, the victim of my RH negative blood status. My complications from an enlarged afterbirth caused me to have convulsions, fall off the bed, and severely bite my tongue. It was exactly the day of our fifth wedding anniversary. I eventually awoke, my head and body aching, looking straight ahead to the foot of the bed, to a sullen and teary-eyed husband just standing there, trying to smile, holding a small narrow-neck porcelain vase with straw flowers inside. Our fourth child, Jean Michel, was delivered by caesarian section in April 1958. Not having had to come through the birth canal, but simply having been lifted from the warm inhabitation of the past eight months, his head was perfectly formed; he was beautiful and remains so. Future babies would have to be taken by caesarian section prematurely as I could not go full-term because of my RH factor.

Two years later, I gave birth to a little girl who was stillborn. One year later, baby number six, our *girl*, finally arrived. My red-blood-cell levels were checked weekly and all precautions had been taken to remove this child by caesarian section when levels became dangerous. Tests showed it had to be done when I was only seven months along. There she was, not really completely finished, weighing only two pounds, and keeping her alive was now the question. Remember, this was 1961! A few months later, pediatrician Doctor Joe said that he was asked to speak about Lisa, our little "miracle baby" at a convention in Chicago. He said to Al and me, "Not just ordinary doctors, you know, but surgeons and specialists from throughout the country." He said no one believed him: "With that baby having so many complications, so premature, a severely low red blood count, a damaged spleen, unable to digest her food, and having to go through a total blood replacement, it was not possible." We wanted her, and she wanted us. I never doubted at her birth that she would pull through. Lisa had a fortitude of spirit, which continues to carry her even through today. Babies number seven and eight, little boys, delivered prematurely by caesarian section, died shortly after birth.

## Granddaughter Victoria's Eulogy

My thoughts came back to where we were, in church; Al's ashes were in a small black box on the altar, just above the large bouquet from "the Harem." Granddaughter Victoria began to speak:

"While my mother and I were staying with my grandparents in Narragansett, my mother overheard a conversation between them which she in turn, relayed to me. Meme was standing in front of the mirror. Pepe was lying on the bed. She was trying on a shirt and asks my pepere, 'Al, does this shirt look all right?' and he says 'Yes, Aline, that looks nice.' 'Well, I don't know,' she says, 'It's like dressing up an elephant, and in the end it's still an elephant.' Al looks at her, 'Stop making fun of my sweetheart!' Fifty-five years together and still in love!"

Victoria continued: "They were, as Meme said, senior citizen Romeo and Juliet. You stand in line at the checkout at the supermarket, and see the little booklets on marriage and relationships, all of which have an underlying theme, stating that 'everyone must work at getting along with their partner or spouse, because there are no perfect relationships or marriages.'

"Bull! I do believe my grandparents officially prove that wrong! I have almost no memories of one without the other. Life is but a series of memories. They spent their lives together, for I have no memories of them apart. What are we, if not those memories that others have of us when we are no longer present and have passed on? Every memory that I have of my grandparents is filled with warmth and caring, unconditional and unfathomable love.

"I was about four years old. I had been given a stick horse for Christmas, one of the good ones, where you press the ears and it whinnies. So I mounted my steed, made sure my father wasn't looking, and headed off down the road from my house to my grandparents' house alone! My father wasn't too happy with me, needless to say, but you know, Pepe was just a whole lot more fun! I later blamed the stick horse. It was definitely his fault. I was simply guilty by association.

"Pepe showed me how to get to the candy in the top drawer of the dresser. Jason can relate with me on this one. You pull out the bottom drawer, then the next above, and make steps. Very sneaky. There were always the little orange candies in the tin can. And then, there were airplane rides on the feet. He and Jack would lie on their backs with their feet in the air and I'd lie on their feet. They'd hold my hands, and I'd go for a ride! They'd make a bargain with me. 'If we give you airplane rides, will you give us back rubs?' I'd say 'maybe,' absolutely certain not to tie myself down to any obligations, and I'd of course scamper away at the end.

"Jack and Pepe were my playmates when I was little, and now they are my guardian angels. I am lucky enough that, as I continue my life, I have two angels watching over me. It seems that sweet sixteen has been bittersweet sixteen. On October 1, I was on my way to my homecoming dance. On October 8, I was on my way to be with Meme because my grandfather has passed on. Life is wonderful and horrible, and has a way of taking you places that you did not expect to go, nor were you ready to go. It is a hard lesson to learn, that you cannot fix or change yesterday but that you can only look to tomorrow. As Meme said (and I do not remember the source of the quote), when you are in bed with sorrow, happiness is waiting at the foot.

"Meme, my grandfather, although we cannot see him physically, is certainly sitting beside you, because you are and will always be his beautiful queen. You have taught me that there is reason for everything, and to look at every day with optimism and hope. And I want to thank you for that. I want to thank you for being there for me, and for sharing your husband and my grandfather, Albert Coutu, with me.

"One of the dearest memories I have of you both is of you singing together."

*Looking at my beautiful sixteen-year-old granddaughter, standing there so poised, I was reminded of one of the songs Al and I would sing,*

*"Sunrise, Sunset" from Fiddler on the Roof. "When did she get to be a beauty, When did he grow to be so tall, Wasn't it yesterday when they were small." The melody rang through my head, and I thought back upon what had been.*

Victoria continued, "My grandfather loved nothing more, Meme, than to hear you play. 'Isn't it beautiful,' he would say.

"As Martin Luther King said, 'Nothing on Earth is so well suited to make the sad merry, and the merry sad (and) to give courage to the despairing, as music.'" *At this point, in response to Victoria's looking at me and expecting a nod for either "yes" or "no," depending on if I felt I could pull myself together to play, and receiving a "yes" nod, she then said,* "And so, Meme, I invite you to play for I am certain that Pepe is listening."

I knew Victoria would be inviting me to play. I was still in *zombie* mode, but in some way, I needed to give a tribute to the man who had been my entire life. And I did play, without halting, without fear, but as perfectly as I could, as this particular song, "I Will Always Love You" was my tribute to a man who, through sickness and in health, bad times and good times, my multiple surgeries, cancer, and hospitalization for several months with thrombophlebitis, had kept his commitment to love and protect me and to protect our children, and had made my life so full, so exciting, and so happy. The sobs emitting from the congregation were becoming overwhelming, as well as the repeated nose-blowing. I thought my piece was simply too sad and reminiscent of Al and me, as a couple. Then something strange happened. I know not how, as this had never happened before, but I believe I inadvertently hit the "demo" button on the keyboard, and strange, loud instrument noises blasted into the church. Everyone broke into hilarious laughter. I shut off the button, and continued playing. When I finished, I looked up to the left rear corner pew of the church, and saw him there, smiling in approval, as he always had, every Sunday, after I'd played my prelude piece by Chopin, Schubert, or Dvorak, and I do think I detected a wink. I was pleased with myself that I had carried through. It pleased me to think that "Al" had hit that demo button so everyone would laugh. I felt his presence and returned to my pew, dreaming and reminiscing about what our life together had been.

# 1967; Living in Married Student's College Housing

Life went on. Having sold Al's Restaurant, Al had greater goals, and dreamed of starting a chain of restaurants and making his mark, becoming someone his children would be proud of. We both realized that he needed to further his education, and we moved into University of Rhode Island housing for married students at Fort Kearney, on Narragansett Bay. Of the seven other families who had an apartment in our barracks building, only *we* had the credit to get a telephone. This was an eight-party line, with eight families in our building sharing *one* of those eight lines. It was the time of the McCarthy hearings, and chairs were lined up against my living room wall. Students sat there and watched the hearings while waiting for their turn to use the phone. Al worked at whatever he could find to bring in some money: farming, gardening, house painting, holding sheep for shearing, and of course, dealing with nervous-sheep pee! He would sometimes return home smelling like a sewer. I was working also, trying to help out. There were always students in my small apartment; baby Jack had colic and cried a lot, so one day I simply left! That was it! This relationship was over! I left the barracks complex and walked up the hill, walking, walking, to a new life. "That was it! Enough was enough!" I mumbled to myself. Behind me, driving slowly, was Albert, just following. "Come on, Aline, I love you, I can't be without you." I walked and walked, with him following. Finally, tired of walking, I got into the bakery truck, and we drove back home. I never left him again.

Through the years, Al worked for large organizations, being at various times Director of Food Services at a then world-renowned medical rehabilitation center in New England, at Cape Cod Hospital (where the contingency of security and nursing staff for the Kennedy children, John-John and Caroline, who were there to have their tonsils removed, occupied the entire floor of the hospital). While living in Hyannis, I had the sad honor, as organist at St. Francis Xavier, the Kennedy Church, to play a memorial service for the Kennedys in residence, at the passing of Robert Kennedy. The telephone had rung at 5:45 A.M. The church pastor, obviously distressed, said in a hoarse voice that Bobby Kennedy had just been assassinated, and that I was to prepare a proper music program for the morning service.

He asked that I give him five minutes to call Marion Lewis, and that *I* should then call her to determine our music presentation. Marion was eighty-three years old at the time, always resentful that Vista (now known as the Peace Corp) resisted her still-persistent applications to join their group. Lewis Bay in Hyannis, Massachusetts, is named after her family. She always "smelled" like money, really nice. She "looked expensive," arriving in the choir loft wearing *real* pearls and beautiful clothes, and had a voice that sang like a bird. Truly. As instructed, I waited five minutes, then called Marion. We decided on the music we would present. I said to her, "I'm so moved by all this. I liked Bobby Kennedy, and my heart breaks that such a good man is no longer. It's one thing for me to play, but how can you, Marion, such a good friend of Rose Kennedy, keep your voice steady and strong." She said, "I did it for Jack, I think I can do it for Bobby, too." She did, and sang, not as a bird, but as an angel.

Al became, as time passed, the food service director at Boston College. He always simultaneously continued his studies, and finally, seventeen years after starting in this quest, received his bachelor's degree in business management. Continuing on into graduate studies, aspiring to a master's degree in nutrition, he quite often found himself to be the only male in the home economics classes. This was something he didn't mind, as he liked exchanging recipes with the ladies, and the ladies always found him and his little goatee and French accent charming.

Al was a scholar. He always carried a book with him wherever we went. If I was practicing, or shopping, he would read while waiting.

He never rushed me into selecting a new dress or shirt. While I shopped, he would sit reading, close by, so I could ask him what he thought of anything I put up against me from the dress racks. He would look up at me, smile, give a nod of approval, or even shake his head "no." One day, at Marshall's, two ladies had been observing us, and one lady said, "Boy, are you lucky. My husband looks at his watch, points at it, says, 'Look kiddo, you've got thirty minutes...so get going.'" I was so accustomed to his being there with me whenever I turned around, that I had come to take it for granted. Then I replied to the lady, "He cooks as well!" They looked at this cute little man (as he'd been referred to on occasion) and I'm sure they wanted to take him with them.

Al enjoyed dialogue. He was always reading, and I was often amazed at how much he contributed to a conversation about almost anything. He was so intelligent, so bright, and I was so proud listening to him. He especially enjoyed dialogue with people who spoke French. At one time Honey Lane's hay deliveries came from Canada, sixteen tons at a time, via trailer truck. When Francois from the tiny village of Ste. Jeanne d'Arc in Canada, was to arrive, our best room in the house was prepared for him. Al would call it the "Queen Elizabeth Room," as they had at the Queen Elizabeth Hotel in Montreal. After dinner, a meal that Al had prepared with eager anticipation of his friend Francois, who would dine with us, he would light his pipe in the fireplace room, and they would speak French all evening long. The next morning, all available hands at the farm would help Francois unload the hay and stack it in the hay storage area. Al and Francois bade each other great goodbyes. "Au revoir, au revoir," Francois's left arm still waving out of the open truck window as he drove away.

Sadly, there came a time when it would be Francois's last trip, his swan song, as they say. Al's folks were visiting. They had the guest room next to the "Queen Elizabeth" room. Francois arrived with a lady friend, who we knew was not his wife. We'd met his little wife when we had visited their farm in Canada and she was "putting up her stores for the winter." This was not her. This was a very glamorous woman, who wore a great deal of makeup, and who was obviously no farmer's wife, and to add to this entire scene. Francois had had his hair permed! Horrors! At breakfast, Al's dad came up first, saying there was a "lot going on in the room next to mine and Ma's." When Francois and the girlfriend came up, we introduced them to Dad and Ma as Mr. and Mrs. Breakfast conversation was polite but strained.

Next, shortly after the start of the unloading of hay with Buddy French, our barn manager, Buddy stops the whole operation and says "This hay is no good!" Upon opening a few bales, the centers had smoke and dust coming out. If you let the fermenting continue and combustion takes place, you will have a barn burned to the ground! Buddy had all the hay bales returned to the hay truck for reloading. We had no new hay and Francois had no money. We watched our hay being driven away, back to Canada, in the trailer truck. There were no "Au Revoirs" being waved out of the cab window as they left.

About two or three weeks later, Al called Francois's house in Canada to see if he would be coming with a replacement load of hay. His wife answered the telephone, in French, and said, "Francois will never again come to the United States Never!" and hung up. His goose was cooked! Goodbye forever, Francois.

When Al spoke with people, he became "one of them." A bond was formed from the onset. Al had a problem insofar as he would immediately associate himself with the dialect and accent that was being used by the person he was speaking with. Since especially older generations have retained their accents, Al went into conversations in which you would have guessed he was suddenly of Italian birth, or Hispanic birth, or Jewish, any race at all. Just name it and it was Albert! He couldn't help himself. Lisa would scold him, and I would tell him that perhaps people would think he was making fun of them. But it was the opposite; the friendship between speakers evolved, both having the same accent, dialect, gestures, and so forth. He just couldn't help it! One day he was visiting his friend Dr. Jorge Scott, who was in the hospital. Dr. Scott was from Cuba and had a Hispanic accent. Things went well for a while. Then two other doctors came in to visit with Dr. Scott. One was Jewish and the other mid-Asiatic. They would speak among themselves, each with their own personal accent, but then, when all three started speaking together with Al, and all three accents were in progress, he tried to keep up, going from one to the other. Within a rather short period of time, Al, now very confused, excused himself, saying, "Aline will be waiting for me at home. I must say goodbye."

At a Jewish wedding at the Mount Washington Hotel in Bretton Woods, New Hampshire, in 2004, Al was given the traditional yarmelka to wear on his head. He wore the yarmelka and, resembling several of the older participants in the group, he became one of them. I found him on several occasions in deep conversation with Jewish gentlemen. The conversations would end with, "Shalom, my friend! Shalom." "Now then," Al said to me, knowing that at the time of his birth, it was not a practice to circumcise Christian male babies, "if anyone follows me to the latrine in the men's room, I'm sunk!"

## Chef Albert Food Products: Early-Mid Sixties

Al was considered to be an "entrepreneur," never letting the grass grow under his feet, but always looking ahead to success. In addition to managing the kitchen at the West Warwick Country Club and catering parties for the Elks, Rotary, etc., he began Chef Albert Food Products from our little barn to the rear of our house. He and a helper would make meat pies and fruit pies—the fruit pies individually bagged with bright labels called "Jewel Gems" in flavors of apricot, lemon, apple, blueberry, etc. The pies were delivered to bars and small stores in the area. One day, the phone rang, and Al, elbow-deep in flour and filling mix, took the call. The man started with, "How are you?" Al said, "I'm damn busy so you'd better hurry up and tell me what you want." "Well, I'm Mr. Antoine. I'm the buyer for the Almacs chain of supermarkets. I've just had one of your meat pies at Jim's Place, and I would like you to service my stores with your pies." Before long we were supplying every major chain in Rhode Island, except A & P, then got our federal inspection approval, moved to a larger location in Providence, and serviced stores in Massachusetts and other parts of New England.

We were making pizzas for Hi-Hat Food delivery trucks, supplying the Kennedy Butter & Eggs stores and hospitals with portion-controlled meals, bulk meatloaf, etc. The business came to the point that our receivables became so great that with the span of time between purchase of ingredients, manufacturing, packing, and delivery of product, then waiting six weeks for payment, we began selling our receivables and the squeeze became too tight. We were refusing new orders as we could not subsidize the purchase of raw ingredients. At a great loss, we sold our inventory, equipment, and customer list to Hi-Hat foods. At least five years later, while on vacation in Maine, we found a "Chef Albert Pork Pie" in the freezer case of a small grocer. Al asked about it. The owner said, "Oh, those are just great! They go like hotcakes!" Can you imagine? That pie had been in their freezer for five years! It was all we could do not to burst out laughing.

# State Fairs

✳ During the early Chef Albert days, when Marc and Jack were ten to twelve to fourteen years old, and Mike five to six to seven years old, we would reserve booth space and bring our products to state fairs in Rhode Island, Connecticut, and Massachusetts. It started with Al building a ten- by ten-foot booth, which he'd priced out at sixty-seven dollars for construction materials. Close, but no cigar! The inside would hold the refrigerator, two stoves, and preparation areas, and the outside of the building would have long boards attached as seats, where customers could sit and eat. Every time he thought construction was terminated, the building would leak, but worse, if one or two diners got up on one side, the structure would tip over, going up on that side, and down on the other! So, every time someone approached wanting to sit down, everyone at the counter would have to rise, and all would sit down at the same time. The same thing would happen if one or two people were leaving. To correct this, more and more money went into the booth, and with help from construction people who knew what they were doing, the actual cost of the booth totaled out at $650.

There were two ovens, each with two shelves in the booth, with signs indicating each kind of specialty pie within. Canadian meat pie, pork pie, beef pies, and kosher pie. He'd obey the request of each customer and pull the pie out of the door of choice, but of course, they were all the same kind of pie.

Our stock of Chef Albert meat pies were kept in our refrigerated truck nearby. They were the pies which were returns from the markets we delivered to, that is, they were not sold at the time the new delivery arrived. They were fine and selling them at the fairs was a perfect way of reducing our losses. Marc and Jack had one or two friends who hung around the entire time of the fair. They would go to the truck and bring back pies when we needed restocking. One time, one of Jack's twelve-year-old buddies hollered out as they were approaching with their large case of pies. "Hey, Mr. Coutu, here's the last of the stales!" Oh my goodness. I wondered what the customers sitting at our booth and eating one of our pies thought!

Marc and Jack enjoyed the fairs, especially at Rocky Hill in Rhode Island. They would help owners feed and water their stock, do errands for them, walk the animals, and in turn, receive tickets for free rides on the merry-go-round, ferris wheel, etc., which they would use when not helping us in the booth. Mike's penchant, at age five and six, was more exploratory and you would know pretty much where he was as the show announcer would bellow into the loud-speaker, "Would the little boy with a striped shirt and blue shorts please remove himself from the bull ring, or as the case might be, "remove himself from the show ring," or from "interfering with the sheep demonstration." Name it and Mike was in the middle of it. To this day, he still is.

To our horror, Mike had gathered up the Blue Ribbon winners of tomatoes, potatoes, and whatever other vegetables were in the judging competition, and brought them back to us. He would say, "Oh no, they have them right out there so people can take them for free." Back to their rightful owners they went...with apologies! The exhibiting farmers had to watch their bunnies or chickens when Mike was around. After seeing him being chased by three boys much older and larger than he, with a rabbit firmly clutched in his arms, we decided the fair was not the place for Mike. We left him home with a sitter after that.

One of the fairs which we were sold a bill of goods on, and told that we would have a great, central spot, and the money would come in profusion, was at the Big E, the Eastern States Exposition, in western Massachusetts. This super sales person with green teeth, and a gun in his belt, convinced us that the spot he was subleasing to us would be terrific, and that we would split the profits. Sounded good, and off we went. There was the refrigerated truck, pulling an eighteen-foot house trailer which had a kitchen, well set up for food preparation, with a bedroom in the rear for the boys. Al and his brother had cut 6' openings along one side of the trailer to use as serving counters. I drove our car and pulled a small pop-up trailer where Al, Lisa, age two, and I would sleep.

The spot was lousy, right behind the cow barn. Elephants and huge animals would pass directly in front of our booth, making the largest droppings we'd ever seen. Backwoods people, the ladies wearing satin turbans with fake pony tails, trod through these mega-pies until they were flattened out. There was no business. Everyone came to see the shows and exhibits in the central exhibit hall, and it was nowhere near us. We suffered a total loss. Although Al and I worried about it, the boys loved the fair, and had a terrific time exploring every avenue of the Big E.

At the end of the last day, we slept uneasily at the fairgrounds. All through the night, exhibits were being broken down, and animals, people, and trucks were moving. We awoke to find ourselves absolutely alone on these acres of tar. But then, what would we do about paying the green-teeth guy? And there he was, out there, coming towards us. How could we explain that there had been no profits, and would he share the losses? Nope, that won't go over well! Al gave me the signal to jump into the car, it pulling the pop-up, and he and the boys jumped into the truck, pulling the trailer, with the ovens still plugged in, and made a dash for the gate, plugs, wires, and sparks popping and flying off the back end in celebration of a clean break-out! Phew! We never went back there again.

# New England Medical Rehabilitation Center

✳ In the summer of 1977, we found ourselves unemployed. The rehabilitation center came under new management, along with new department heads. Most of the department heads we had worked with were also let go. After several years of being there, it was not easy to accept, as we had loved the work, the patients, and our involvement in an environment of hope for a better life for those many who came to us for help. As Director of Food Services, Al fed the hundreds of clients and staff three meals daily, became involved with state programs, and initiated a school lunch program that included not only handicapped children, but the many children who attended a school for the deaf. In addition, there was vocational rehabilitation for adults, and a medical/ nursing division for post-stroke, post-accident patients. Al arranged for special meals where needed, party fare when requested, and would meet me for a late lunch telling me about all the great stories of events that had taken place in the kitchen or dining room earlier in the day.

One day, he watched as one little deaf boy started signing (sign language) to another deaf boy at the other end of the room, and then the other boy would send his message back by his hand signals. It didn't take too long that one boy got up, walked across the room, and punched the other boy in the nose! They had been arguing, but how could Al have known? He didn't know sign language! Al was laughing so hard, that he was telling me this while wiping the tears of laughter on his face. He'd get such a kick out of watching and being with the kids, and they all liked Al, too. We met the requirements of having some of those handicapped children in our home, and there were weekends that we had a young visitor or two with us. When Gary Costinuic, who was autistic, was given a fly swatter to kill some flies, we found him outdoors, swinging away. He said there were "more out there." One time, when Gary was holding Geno, our Canadian Draft pony, with a lead while Al was cleaning out Geno's hooves, Gary had slowly edged Geno towards the electric fence. Just about the time Al got to the right rear hoof, Geno's nose hit the electric fence and Al was kicked right into the air, and landed about eight to ten feet away. A few expletives occurred at that time, and Al had such a swelling on his right thigh that we had to cut away his pant legs to get them off. That purple and blue bruise, with a hoof mark clearly defined, lasted for quite some time.

Kiddos in wheelchairs needed special attention, but we managed. I had started at the Medical Rehab Center as Director of Admissions, then took on the funding for all programs, therapies, equipment, and wheelchairs. We both felt, because of our devotion and involvement, that we truly mattered. There were many admirable people on staff, and we were proud to be part of that team, and that was a good feeling. Many years later, an unbelievably handsome and grown Gary Costinuic came to our house to visit. He had learned at the center how to control his handicap, had a huge smile, was now married, and seemed happy and content with his life.

So now we were becoming victims of downsizing! What to do? We had not been prepared for the firings. No advance notice, no two-weeks notice. Al was told, "You are being terminated today. Thank you for your services, but here's your jacket and your briefcase, and do not go back to your kitchen. Just leave."

Al, being keener than I, had sensed mischief was at hand for several days, and he knew something would be happening, but what? His head chef had conspired with the new powers that be, that he could simply take over the kitchen, since Al had everything so well organized, his programs, federal requirements, menus, etc., that, without skipping a beat, all would go on as they had "pre-Al." But the plotters had missed something: how popular Al was with all the staff, especially the girls. That morning, the human resources secretary called the new president's secretary, who then called Al's secretary, and told her of the plot. "Al would be called for a meeting, fired, and would then be escorted directly to his car." Al was always quick. Though acting surprised when called into President Church's office, and seeing that he'd been followed by a "henchman" carrying his jacket and briefcase, and then escorted directly to his car, he wondered how long it would take them to realize that he had shredded every file, every program, every menu, staffing, federal regulations, etc., that morning, and the filing cabinets were totally empty!

The head chef was known as a "brown-noser." He knew nothing. He could not possibly recreate files and records that Al had worked on and assembled over seven dedicated years. Then, when it was discovered by the chef's wife, and related to the center's president, that her husband was sleeping with the young boys from the school for the handicapped that he was bringing home, this scandal, added to his ignorance in being able to put together the dining services as they had been, had him fired and he too, was "out in the cold." Sad but true. I was told I was no longer needed when I returned to work after being away two weeks to be at my father's side when he passed away, and having helped my mother with funeral arrangements and post-burial financial matters. Nice touch, I would say! I do suspect that Al's paper-shredding coup helped them a little in that decision.

## Woodsmen and Entertainers

✳ It was summer of 1976. Life needed to move along, but to where, we simply didn't know. Al reinitiated his bachelor's degree program in taking courses at Franklin Pierce College, and I took business classes at Nathaniel Hawthorne three nights a week. We surveyed our situation, took stock of our few assets and enthusiastic capabilities, and decided we could earn income by cutting some of the trees on our 100 acres of farm land and selling cordwood. Al purchased the needed equipment to cut and split the wood, and traded in the car towards an old 350 Ford truck which would be used for deliveries. What luck, exactly when there was an embargo on fuel oil, we were in the cordwood business.

Through late summer and early fall, until the snow began, Al and a helper sawed down hundreds of trees, cutting and splitting them, and then loading them on the truck. Arriving at the delivery point, there was the unloading and stacking to be done at the customer's house. That was a lot of work. I would now and then go with him to unload and stack, and very often, we would spend the rest of the evening with the clients, huddled around their cozy fireplace, drinking wine, and making friends.

Several memories of my "woodsman" seep into my thoughts. One day, out back working alone, he'd cut a tree which was of formidable size. As it cracked and began falling, Al had not noticed the rather large branch protruding from it. Bang! When Al came to, he searched for his glasses, collected himself, and came home to report the incident. Here stood before me, my hero and my lover, dazed, eyeglasses askew, with a bump of some considerable size beginning to loom on the side of his head. I sat him down, straightened out his glasses, put an ice pack on his head, gave him lots of sympathy, and insisted that he lie down for a little while. He resisted this forced "time off," but complied, especially when I said I would lie with him and hug him for awhile.

Another time, his helpers, sons Marc and Jack, had left and Al persisted in his task of cutting trees in an area which would eventually become a turnout for the horses. Right around dinnertime, the three he'd been sawing fell right onto the electric wires. Lights went out in the neighborhood for as far as the eye could see. Anyone within a mile who was trying to prepare supper was in deep trouble. I thought, *so is Al!* With this fertile mind of his, he quickly stepped into mode, cutting the tree and branches down, piece by piece, from the bottom up, fireplace size, and they came to lie right there at his feet. When the repair crew appeared on the scene, Al, the culprit, looking innocent and unknowing, hollered: "Hey! What the hell is going on? My wife says there's no electricity at the house!"

Another one: Marc appeared at the house, looking as though he was about to faint. He'd been cutting wood with his father, and Al's saw slipped, and cut the leather boot Marc was wearing. I had Marc sit on the toilet seat. He said he felt weak. I said, "Bring your head down and hold it between your hands." I removed the boot, and sure enough, the saw had gone through the leather, and had a slice of Marc's leg looking like hamburger. I reached for the first-aid kit across the hall and heard a crash. Marc had fainted, not to the front, but to the side, in back of the bathroom door, still in a seated position, and his head and body were bedecked with panties and pantyhose which had been drying behind the door. I looked at my first-born, this beautiful, rugged man, with muscles of Hercules, lying there with my faun-shaded, size medium, K-Mart undies. It would have been too much for my macho man to come to with me laughing, so I muffled one or two giggles. With an ice pack on his head, and some soft, loving chatter from me, Marc awoke, a little stunned, and I patched him up. To this day, Marc will show that chainsaw scar to anyone who asks!

In the meantime, during early summer, I had been approached by Mario Cossa, a teacher at Keene State College, and a performer, as well. He said that the Keene County Club had just recently completed their new dining room/lounge, and wanted Mario and his troop to perform there on Fridays and Saturdays on a weekly basis. He wanted me to join them until his usual pianist returned from England in the fall. That was great. Rehearsals were held at our house (while Al was out back cutting wood). There were traveling performers from Canada, so charming, so delightful, so beautiful, and so talented. Friday and Saturday evenings, Al would get the dirt out from around his nails and knuckles, and would go with us to the country club. Al really "cleaned up nice" and he joined us with the singing where he could. He constantly amazed me with his strength and determination, and the fun he was to be with, even after a hard day of chopping wood. I just loved and admired him, and besides, I had found myself a free tenor! The performers liked me, and I liked them, and I was asked to stay on as pianist/singer until Christmas, when the club would be closing for the winter months.

One night, while we were rehearsing before mealtime, people were lined up to come in for dinner. We were practicing music from "The Sound of Music" which would be part of our repertoire that evening. Two tall gentlemen with light sandy hair, a woman, and a young boy came into the lounge where we were, sat on the fireplace hearth, introduced themselves, and began singing with us. When they went in for dinner, I asked Mario and one of the girls, "Did you catch their names? I didn't." After their dinner, while we were now performing, the four came again and sat on the hearth, smiling, shaking our hands again, and joined in the singing. We were embarrassed that we didn't know the names they had given us earlier. Mario whispered in my ear while I was playing, "Aline, I think they are the VonTrapps," so he simply asked them, "Are you the VonTrapps?" "Yes" was the answer. One brother, a physician and his wife, had picked up the second brother, who is a professor in Boston, and they were just passing through Keene, New Hampshire, on their way to Stowe, Vermont, to visit their mother, Maria VonTrapp. We sang with gusto and pride. What a treat to have the VonTrapps joining us in songs about their family, as they intensely recalled their early days of adventure and courage.

Until the following year, 1977, when I returned to work at Wayne Green Publications as Advertising Director, we were living on very little income. We had so enjoyed the past months and were truly happy, and it had been like the miracle of the "fish and the loaves on the mount" whereas each time I would pay bills, etc, the checkbook always seemed to replenish itself and I would have enough there for the "next round."

*Honey Land Farm:*
A Quarter Century of Great Riding Adventures;
Meeting New Friends, Several Prominent, from Everywhere;
Good Food; Wonderful Times; Funny Times; and Some Sadness

✳ "There's a real nice little house on Goldmine Road in Dublin that's just come on the market. They're asking $19,500 for it," Terry, the real estate lady said. "It's easily worth another four or five thousand dollars, but the present owner has been transferred to another state. I'd really hurry if I were you. I've got at least four other prospects ready to pounce on this place." I said, "I'll meet you there in thirty minutes..." and there it was. Just very quaint, a dual-level house with central entry; five steps up and you were in the living room, the kitchen was straight ahead, and the bath, master bedroom, and dressing room were on the right. Taking five steps down at the entry, the garage was on the left, the utility room straight ahead, and two bedrooms on the right.

"I'll take it," I said and gave her a deposit. That night, when Al had returned from the medical center and we were having dinner, I told him of the nice little house we'd just bought. "What do you mean, a little house we've just bought?"

"It was a terrific deal, convenient for Lisa's school," I told him, "It's not a fixer-upper. It's perfect as it is. Lets go see it." He did, and we moved in shortly afterwards. We were both working. Al as director of food services at the center, and I, as advertising manager at Wayne Greene Publishing. Actually, as the years passed, there were many, many additions to the house, a new large glassed-in porch/family room with fireplace, a new wood deck that the boys finished hammering away at the day of Lisa's high school graduation party, with people speaking above and Marc and Jack hammering underneath. The garage eventually became a very charming guest room with eight-foot glass sliding doors replacing the garage door.

Lisa was eight years old, coming on nine, when we moved in. Many of her friends at the Dublin Elementary School had ponies, and some had joined the local Pony Club. "Can you buy me a pony," became the standard of the day. "Melissa has a pony, Terry has a pony." One day, on a whim, we'd seen an advertisement that someone just outside Concord had two ponies for sale. We got the address, and drove there. In a very, very small, very, very dirty stall, stood two ponies, almost chest-high in manure. Everything was filthy, and the smell of urine overwhelming. One pony was a honey-colored mare, and the other a black, hyper stallion. So, here we were, looking over two small ponies. How could this happen? All we had was our car, and absolutely no way to transport a small mare. We had no supplies, no hay, none of the items necessary to care for an animal. There was no question about it. Lisa wanted the mare. Her name was Miss Buttons. Lisa, who hated parks where animals are caged or restricted to certain small areas, mostly on concrete, insisted that Miss Buttons could not possibly stay where she was. We paid the owner fifty dollars in cash, and assessed our situation.

We rented a U-Haul trailer and a temporary hitch. Into the trailer went two bales of hay, Miss Buttons, and son, Mike. His job was to put the mare at ease, talk to her, and let her know that she wasn't alone in the box on wheels. It was now dark, and beginning to snow. When we stopped at red lights, Al would lower the window, and call to the back, "Hey Mike, everything okay in there?" and the box would answer back, "Yep, everything's fine." Other stopped drivers looked at us in a very bewildered manner.

When we arrived home, there was no other place for Miss Buttons but to put her into our garage. Therefore, the occupants on that lower level were Mike, Lisa, and Miss Buttons. Three bedrooms, three people, sort of. After a little while, the old Bond's corner store building was being sold. We bought one-half of the store, which would become a barn, and someone else bought the other one-half to serve as their dog kennel.

Somewhere in there, we bought Geno. He was beautiful, rugged, and looked like a small draft (work) horse. Geno could carry a two hundred-pound rider or, harnessed to a whiffletree and chains, could pull felled trees out into a loading area. After the "new" barn was rebuilt into six stalls, plus a tack room, Miss Button and Geno resided there together. In the morning, we would place a halter on each horse, and lead them to the turnout area out back.

We had a little dog named Duchess. Lisa was about ready to leave for something special that her Girl Scout troop was doing that day. Al had breakfast ready for Duchess, and was calling her name. I looked out the back window, to where Miss Buttons and Geno were, and I noticed extra legs to the other side of the mare. I said to Al, "Oh, Duchess is out back just to the other side of Miss Buttons." Al replied, "No, she isn't. She's right here in the kitchen." Well, whose dog then is to the other side of the mare?" We opened the back door, and each of us, Al, Lisa, Mike, and myself, took slow, deliberate steps up the incline and towards the enclosure. We stared in disbelief. Geno, not moving a step, was staring too, having a look as though he was in big trouble.

To the other side of Miss Buttons, now to be known as Mrs. Buttons for propriety's sake, stood the sweetest, most adorable pony foal. She was honey-colored, having kept her mother's coat color, and not at all darker, considering the sire had been that black pony stud back in Concord. We named her "Honey." That adorable unexpected miracle was actually the beginning of Honey Lane Farm. Although Honey later died in an accident, we will always remember her sweet face, tiny legs, and how she played with us as if she were a puppy.

# We go to the Bank for Construction Money

With creative financing, and including our unemployment checks as income, we prepared a thirty-four-page presentation for the bank. We'd researched the horse market throughout our area and beyond. The University of Vermont had recently introduced programs in equine care, record keeping, and management. The blacksmith said that "where he'd been to clients with one horse three years ago, now those same people had three horses." There were eighteen equestrian publications on the market. Horses were no longer considered "the sport of kings" for the wealthy, and a healthy market for boarding stables, buyers and sellers of horses, blacksmith services, etc., was growing by leaps and bounds. We developed our presentation to the bank into projections of not only horse boarding, but of training, residential childrens' summer camps, and adult riding camps. After the bank's blessing, and the near-necessary loan, our riding programs, through the years, went beyond the proposal.

Marc, our architect, had begun designing this massive structure while still in the employment of Universal Studios. The building would be 180 by 80 feet in size. It would contain 27 stalls, a 60- by 120-foot indoor arena, a tack (saddlery) room, a glassed-in overhead viewing lounge, and enough storage space for the 90 tons of hay which would come in during the year, 16 tons per trip, via a 16-wheeler truck from Canada. Poised and handsome, and having won a State Debating Championship while in high school, Marc was best qualified to present our plans and request permits, to the Dublin Selectmen, Planning Board, and to the public. My husband, Al, a sometimes temperamental little Frenchman, having shown his dislike for people who thought they could run his affairs, would wisely be kept "behind the scenes." Permits were granted and Al, Marc, and Jack went to work!

Wood for construction would come from the trees on our property. The cut trees were then hoisted up by a cherry picker onto the sawmill owner's truck, and then off to the mill for Al, Marc, and Jack to saw into boards. Several publications, including *Yankee Magazine*, came to take pictures and wrote about these "modern day pioneers" as referred to by Fritz Weatherbee, well-known reporter and speaker.

The work began; 64-foot trusses, required to span the ceiling area of the arena, were delivered by truck. Marc and Jack dug 6-foot holes into the ground every 12 feet, and placed in each, 20-foot high posts and beams. As each of these tall posts and beams were put in place, the skyscape became more and more interesting. Folks would pull their cars up, and sit and watch in fascination. If they were fascinated at this stage, they were in for more excitement. With the help of a crane, the 64-foot trusses were hoisted up and the boys would grab each truss as it came, straighten it out, and lay it to rest atop the roof foundation they'd prepared. The grand finale was watching my "gymnasts" hop from truss to truss while strapping each truss to the next.

Throughout the summer months, construction continued, and a ribbon-cutting ceremony was held with Rob Trowbridge, president and CEO of *Yankee Magazine* and its affiliated publications, officiating. He was a good friend and neighbor, as well as a terrific banjo player, and we'd done some pretty nice music together on occasion.

My small ad in *Yankee Magazine*, "See the New England Foliage on Horseback," would receive amazing response, and details of riding at Honey Lane were mailed out, accompanied by itineraries. We started on a small scale, having at the beginning, simple overnight accommodations in the former Little Barn, and upstairs in the loft. After the construction of our lodge in 1985, detailed, enticing itineraries, with the lodge as home base, would be mailed out with the following letterhead:

Honey Lane Farm Equestrian Stables and Lodge
*"A Touch of Europe in the Heart of New England."*

Al and I had ridden abroad on several occasions. It was our intention to duplicate as closely as possible the riding that we would offer. The day-by-day itineraries for "The 7-day Mount Monadnock Ride," "The Inn-to-Inn Monadnock Highlands Trek," and the "Heart of New England Riding Holiday" were mailed out as part of our "media pack." We also offered "on premises" riding packages for adult beginners, with short country walk-trot rides during the last two or three days of their stay.

Everyone who came to Honey Lane did so after having completed the application and filled in detail their riding abilities, experience, and instructors' names and telephone numbers. Riding at Honey Lane, on horses that were well trained, many of them state and New England champions, was not at all like the movies everyone has seen, such as "City Slickers." We rode English style, with England saddles, and that was standard fare. Honey Lane became truly, a five-star Equestrian Facility and our clientele would come from many states in the USA, and many countries abroad including England, France, Japan, and Germany. Those wanting to ride Western came with their own horses and tack. As a matter of fact, eight ladies who rode in the annual Rose Bowl parade, sent eight to ten huge boxes with their Western saddles, etc., ahead of their arrival. For these ladies, we used some of our horses who'd originally come to us as "Western broke."

The first years, before the lodge was built in 1985, residential riders would sleep in the "Little House," our former first barn, transformed into a dorm accommodating eight to twelve people, as well as upstairs in the barn, set up to also accommodate the same number. Sleep areas were partitioned off, with curtains along the front of each little room. Sinks for washing were in that dorm, and the outhouse was outdoors, obviously.

God forbid that one or two male riders found themselves staying in the dorm with a bevy of females. Sheer negligees and Victoria's Secret lingerie would strut over to the communal sink, to the embarrassment of the single male, who would wait, and wait, and wait, until all the giggling and girl talk had stopped so that he, too, could avail himself of the wash sink. Almost without fail, the girls, having "laid low," would hop out of their cubicles with flashlights in hand and tease this person (usually one who lived with his mother) but would make it up to him the following night when he was literally forced to attend the country dance in Milford with them. Our male guest would be the envy of all other males, as he was danced around the floor with these "girls" of all ages, each taking turns dancing with him. His "dance card" was full to overbrimming! At the Honey Lane going-away party, a single male, having come alone, would, with great embarrassment, be pinned with a decorated Kotex pad, saying "First Place Winner." How many of you gals out there, reading this, remember those weekends? It did break the ice.

# Girl Scouts and Summer Camp

✳ During shoulder season, that is, mid-March to early June, and November and early December, we offered a weekend Horse Lover's program to Girl Scouts, whereby they would earn their Horselover's badge. These Girl Scout troop reservations were made months in advance. We had the privilege of teaching these up-and-coming members of society, now surely grown and having children of their own, the basic principles of care and love involved with horse ownership. A portion of the Scouts' introduction to Honey Lane and horses was to tell them the story about little Honey, whose name we'd taken as the farm name. The pony, while only five months old, was killed by a speeding driver and we showed the area in the "lane" where that accident occurred. I would tell them that Honey was about the size of a large dog, and Pepe (Al) would sit on the floor in the little barn, with Honey straddled over his legs while he hugged her. I would also show them the tiny yellow halter, hanging on the wall, which had been hers.

Emotions were beginning to build, and when I reached the point and showed them where she was buried by the large rock, out-and-out sobbing began. If they hadn't been too excited about having to actually do a horse program, cleaning stalls, picking up "poops," grooming, as well as riding, to get their badge, this produced immediate converts, and the program was enthusiastically embraced.

*Louise*

✳ One morning Mike, a mental wizard, always having the prize-winning science exhibit while a youngster in school, and having devised a way that visiting parents had to insert coins into his exhibit to have it work, knew absolutely nothing about horses, except that they managed to break fencing and kicked out stall doors, a matter to which he was now tending. Over the intercom, at the house, I heard a frantic Mike calling me to say that the "Dublin School students are here for their riding lessons," and "Lisa isn't back yet." I said, "Michael, greet them, tell them that they are to get their grooming kits, go into their horse's stall (they would know which of our horses they used for their lesson), groom, and tack them up." "Okay." All was quiet for a little while. I kept watching for Lisa to return. The intercom buzzed again. Michael said: "Lisa's not here, and the kids are all on their horses and circling around in the indoor ring. What now?" "Okay Michael, look as though you know what you're doing. Tell them that they are, first, to walk and warm up their horses. If you watch as they go around, tell them 'keep your heels down, and keep your elbows close to your body.' Scrutinize them closely, and they'll think for certain that you're one of the instructors," I replied.

Minutes passed...ten...fifteen...I wondered how long he could keep these youngsters, all much more accomplished than he, occupied with simple position corrections. He didn't call me back. I presumed Lisa had returned and taken over. A while later, Mike came to the house and said, "You know, that new lady in the barn who just brought her horse over here to board?" I had just returned from Florida, where I'd been for several weeks, and really didn't know whom he was speaking about. Mike said, "Well, she's blonde and real pretty and wears a knit hat down over her ears, and she came over to me, offered to take over the class, and is now out there teaching the kids." A lifesaver, I thought, but who is she?

Each year, during "down season" Al and I would leave the farm and head south, in mid-to-late January until mid-March when Girl Scout Horselover programs would resume. While we were in Boynton Beach, an arrangement we'd negotiated with Susan and Stan Horcharik, in trade for their riding holidays at Honey Lane, Jan Gorski, the secretary, had called to say there was a lady who wanted to bring her horse in that day to board. I said, "Today? We don't do things like that. Who is she, what kind of horse does she have, has he been vetted, does he have his negative Coggins, does she have references?"

Jan replied, "She says you know her, that she sells you cards, on consignment, at the Hunting Horn."

"Oh, sweet little thing, I remember her. She's very pleasant, but does she understand the requirements of the vet check, etc., and the finances involved here? She needs to come up with one month's security deposit, and the first and last months of boarding. That's nearly one thousand dollars. Can she come up with that much?"

"Yes, she says she okay with that, and she's given Janie Tuckerman among two or three other references of our boarders, and she wants to be able to be here, and ride with them."

"Well Jan, do this up right. You know how close our budget is, and we can't afford to take a loss on this arrangement." So, Louise and her horse had arrived at Honey Lane about one week before we'd returned from Florida.

So the first I knew of Louise Mellon was that she had rescued Mike and was teaching a riding class in my barn. I called Janie Tuckerman. She said, "Kiddo, are you fooling me? Don't you know who Louise Whitney Mellon is? She could buy you out many times over, anytime." Oh dear. Louise kept three or four of her horses at their estate outside Nashua. She'd brought "Goosebumps," her favorite, to stay with us. Her demeanor and attitude were so kind, so friendly. She seemed as though she'd dropped from heaven.

One evening, several staff members, Al, Lisa, and myself, were invited to dinner at Louise and her husband, Tim's, home. The dining room, beautifully appointed, had large windows and doors leading outside. The bright outdoor lights showed first, the beds of flowers that crowned the house, then hundreds of feet of lawn and greenery, the white fence surrounding the entire property, and the security guards, which were posted at each corner.

Louse invited us to tour the Nottingham racetrack facilities. She kept race horses there, and it was apparent that every person she saw, barn cleaners, groomers, other boarders, really liked her. She would be greeted with warm smiles and they'd call her Louise, not Ms. Whitney, a notable in her own right, not Mrs. Mellon, just "Louise." In her muckers and little beat-up hat, she'd put herself right in with everyone else.

We had dinner in the clubhouse. She reserved a box, from where we could observe the races. However, prior to that, she took us through and introduced us to every person involved with racing and the racetrack, and those in the viewing booths involved with the interstate simulcasting of the races.

At the starting gate, we'd all stood right there, as close as we safely could, feeling underfoot the trembling earth, while the fury of excited huge horses, stomping and rearing, continued on through placement in their box, until the starting bell went off. While there, Louise introduced us to the track veterinarians who told us their role in being track vets, preracing checkups, following horses on the track, and being prepared for an accident.

And an accident did occur. The racetrack was fenced in with white wooden boards, each placed horizontally over the other with an approximate space of twelve inches apart. On one lap, on a curve, one horse had crashed against the top rail of the fence at the point where it connected to the post. The board cracked, the top snapping out and away from the board's bottom, becoming an eight-foot pointed spear, right into a racing lane. One rider, coming in from behind on the left, not seeing the hazard just ahead, rode his horse right into the pointed, piercing spear. Within seconds, the vets and track workers were there and the accident area was covered with a green tarpaulin. The horse was dead and pulled off to the side of the track so the races could continue. It had all happened so fast, and then, handled so discreetly by staff, that if someone had gone away for coffee or to the bathroom, or even chatting together, not paying attention, they would have missed it all. That night, when we left Louise at the track, we were a bit gloomy, on what had been, otherwise, an exciting and uplifting day.

## Christa McAuliffe

✳ Twenty years ago, New Hampshire's "Teacher in Space," Christa McAuliffe, was lost to us forever when the space shuttle Challenger exploded minutes after takeoff. It horrified the entire country and countries abroad. I came to know her husband, attorney Stephen McAuliffe, and their little daughter, Caroline, when Mr. McAuliffe brought her to Honey Lane Farm, enrolling her in our children's summer horsemanship camp. It was important to him that she be in a small, homey-setting. Caroline was tiny, and had the demeanor of a child who needed to gain confidence in those around her. I would comb her hair, wipe her tears when she was sad, turn her over to one of our best and caring counselors, or be there for her anytime she needed comforting. I felt such pride to be holding and rocking the child of a courageous mother, who had given her life in search of an American dream. I felt privileged that this little girl and her father had touched our lives, and, for this short period of time, brought us within their circle. I still think of Caroline. I hear she is now a schoolteacher in Concord.

# Laddie

One particularly very young group of girls came one year, and fell in love with Laddie, one of our smaller ponies. Very shaggy, especially at that time of year, but very gentle and loving. At one point in his grooming I noticed four or five little girls brushing and hugging him, head, ears, tail, back, and tummy! One little girl was lying on the ground directly beneath him. With Laddie, there was no danger in doing this. Exploring while down below, she cried out, "Laddie's a boy! Laddie's a boy!" The other little girls were crying and saying, "No, Laddie's a girl, Laddie's a girl." "Well, come see! Come see! and, pushing each other for a proper look, subjected Laddie to the humiliation of an upside-down viewing from below. It was true! Laddie was a boy.

My principal fear in leaving Honey Lane in November 1996, focused on Laddie, who was forty-two or forty-three years old, shaggy, practically a house pet, but of little more use than being used for grooming and as our exhibit in giving a little course between mares and geldings, female and male horses. What could we do with him? I had fears that a new owner would find him simply one more mouth to feed and to clean up after, and would have him put down. For me, it became almost a panic situation. About one week prior to our scheduled closing of the farm, Pam Godin ran into the house and said, "Can I have Laddie? He's perfect for my three- and five-year-old grandchildren." Thank God! Thank God. My prayers had been answered. Laddie went to live with Pam Godin, an endurance rider as well as our former head trail guide. She was knowledgeable, and an

48

energetic, warm person. Her husband Leo is a gentleman who installs heating systems, and also plays the violin perfectly! Laddie would think he was in heaven.

It was in 2002, when Pam called, saying Laddie was now blind, had trouble getting about, and would not be able to suffer the New Hampshire winter, and she wanted permission to "put him down." He was by then at least forty-eight or forty-nine years old, and I'm sure if there is a horse heaven, he surely had earned top placement for the years of love and caring he'd given all our children. Goodbye Laddie, dear Laddie.

*Christopher*

✳ Losing one of our babies was always difficult. We kept horses who could no longer be ridden, with the "reasoning" that they were "needed for grooming class." Christopher, a 15.2-hands Palomino quarter horse, would sometimes be found in the morning, sitting with his two rear legs extended straight out beneath him and his two front legs in a standing position. The "barn rats" would go into his stall, hug him, reassure him that all was okay, and then, all together, they would pull and get him standing up. Out front of our house, there was a large field which bordered a stand of trees. I believe that during our twenty-five years at the farm, eleven horses who had simply died of old age, or needed to be put down, were buried there, way in the shade of the trees.

# Casper

When our little white pony, Casper, who'd been left with us years ago in lieu of payment of the owner's bills, was very sick and dying, I would go into the barn at night and see Melissa, Lisa's assistant, sitting on the floor of the stall, with Casper's head and little white front legs on her knees, as she hugged and stroked him. Until Casper passed away, Melissa would bring a cot to sleep on so she could stay with him and he would not be alone. I am happy to say that Melissa recently purchased the barn and turnout areas at Honey Lane, and continues her work with horses, teaching and training, at which she always excelled.

*May Queen*

It was winter, and Honey Lane turnouts were perched on hills on the shoulder of Mount Monadnock. May Queen, a handsome roan Percheron Thoroughbred, well along in years, had not been well since an unthinking barn helper walked her outdoors to the top of an icy slope. May Queen's hooves—she was one of the few horses that was shod during the winter months—went out from under her, and she fell on her spine, bumping and banging all the way to the bottom of the hill. She was now limping a great deal. Repeated vet visits, medications, and shots, proved to be of no use; her vision was failing. She was getting old. We have a photo of this exquisite animal competing at Barrington, with "all fours" up and easily clearing a four-foot oxer. She was a champion in every way. Her prowess and awareness for the safety of her rider, when foxhunting, was uncanny. As she moved, cantering and galloping, her head would tip slightly from side to side, and with horses having a normal ninety-degree peripheral vision, she could then see entirely to her rear and assess her field.

We did not know how to bring the matter up to Jeannette Perron, her former owner. She'd purchased May Queen as a foal, and the highlights of her life's experiences had been with this horse she loved so much. She had spent hours and hours riding and talking with her on trails through the woods. Until three or four years prior to this, every week or two, Jeannette would go off in the morning with her May Queen trailering behind the four-wheel drive. Arriving at her fox hunt destination, May Queen's appearance was like no one else's, and was always everyone's favorite.

How could we tell her? No one wanted the responsibility. Those two had been together for over thirty years. In a meeting including Lisa, Al, and myself, we explained to Jeannette that there would be no turning around for this farm favorite. The vet had said that we should put her out of her pain and let her rest with the other horses in our field. Jeannette, now in her early seventies, walked over to the barn and sat and talked with May Queen for quite a while. They talked about their years together, all they'd achieved together, and the happiness she'd brought her mistress. "But now," Jeannette told May Queen, "we need to say goodbye." After a long time, she returned to the house and said, "It's okay, May Queen understands. Go ahead and do it." Of course, there wasn't one dry eye to be seen anywhere.

# Construction of the Lodge

✳ Guests residing in the lodge were in the midst of a master-piece of construction, designed by Marc, and built by Marc, Jack, Mike, our electrician, and Al. From the front door, a visitor was greeted with a slate-floor entry. Raising one's eyes, one saw a crystal chandelier of near-massive proportions, hung from the high open ceiling in line with the catwalk hallway above that ran the full length horizontally across the middle of the living room. There were no supporting beams in the room. Marc had devised a suspension design whereas the second floor, bedrooms, and halls were braced to and held up by the roof. Marc's plan included two stairways, one on either side of the living room, which would serve as a gallery to display a number of paintings and framed horse prints which had been purchased in England. Directly ahead of the foyer was a wide-open carpeted living room, furnished with inviting wingback chairs, and two large couches, end and coffee tables, and lamps to read by. Further along the left wall stood a stately 1830 Jacobean carved chair with a garnet-color velvet seat. Directly beyond the chair was an inlaid game table, which opened up to become a roulette table, purchased during a trip to Italy.

In scanning further along to the left, a Kohler and Campbell console piano was angled away from the wall, making somewhat of a corner with potted greenery and four-foot shrubs behind the piano bench. As the eye traveled from the left wall, and directly to the furthest wall, there was a fireplace midway, with large glass doors on each side leading out to the fourteen-foot-deep by sixty-foot-long balcony, which overlooked the hunt course below. There were two rooms on each side of the living room, with two having direct access to the balcony and the hot tub, which was nearly always occupied. The balcony bedrooms opened onto a second-floor deck, ten by sixty feet long. All bedrooms had baths, were carpeted, and were furnished in Laura Ashley fashion, and had, as in Europe, individually controlled gas heating units.

The lodge was located on a sloping piece of land. Therefore, access to the lower-level dining room, library/TV room, kitchen, and two staff bedrooms was via an entrance to the side of the building. At that entrance, the usual arrival or meeting point after a day of riding was a large welcoming wooden deck, totally encased with flower boxes matching the flower and vine boxes outside the bedroom windows up above. Here is where riders gathered to enjoy a beer or cocktail or two, and discuss the events of the day.

The actual building of this lodge was done in an unusual way. The boys would work on a forty- by sixty-foot wood platform, which they'd laid across the cement foundation they poured. Each section of the lodge, no matter what size, was put together, lying flat, on the wood platform. Marc would carefully measure each frame opening, each window, and on the slanted roof, where the skylights would be placed. When completed, each panel, in turn, would be lifted and secured in place. When it came time to lift these massive, heavy wood wall sections, all hands available in the barn and on the property were called over to help. It was uncanny. Marc's "prefab" walls and roofs slid into place without a fraction of an inch to spare. When finished, the forty- by sixty-foot wood platform would become the floor for the entire lodge. Rear and side decks were added separately.

## Ghosts at the Lodge

✳ *"From ghoulies and ghosties and long leggety beasties, and things that go bump in the night, Good Lord, deliver us!"*

The mention of ghosts at the lodge was quickly cast aside, especially if the report came from one or two ladies who'd spent the night out partying, and had returned to the farm inebriated. Besides, ghosts do not haunt new buildings. But then, the matter became serious. One night, two of our sober riding ladies came running to the farmhouse, approximately 400 feet distance from the lodge. They were screaming, "Mr. Coutu, Mr. Coutu, come quick...there are ghosts in our bedroom!" Al valiantly took hold of a wooden hanger, running behind the ladies back to the lodge, and I was certain he would defend them with his life, if need be.

"Hello? Hello?" We searched everywhere and no ghosts were to be found, so we asked "What did these ghosts look like?" The girls said, "There were two of them, tall and thin, with little caps on their heads."

Al and I stayed around with wooden hangers in hand for awhile, and the ladies eventually went back to bed, with their lights on. On another occasion, one morning, a counselor came to the house, and said I would find the breakfast conversation very interesting were I to go to the lodge dining room. That weekend, we'd had an editor from *Time* magazine in room three, and an editor from *People* magazine in room four. The *People* magazine editor was relating her frightening nighttime experience. She had awakened and found, in the far corner of her room, a tall, thin form, wearing a small cap. The form seemed to be interested in looking at her riding equipment resting on the

56

chair, then over to the bureau, it observed the riding helmet, gloves, crop, etc. She said she was petrified. First, she drew the sheets over her eyes, and then, simply watched! As the form rounded the foot of her bed, going toward the closet where her clothes were hung, she lunged for the figure, hitting her head squarely on the corner of the bathroom wall. A loud thud was heard below in staff sleeping quarters, and two staff members had hurried upstairs to see if something was wrong. I noticed that the editor had a bump on her forehead. I asked her if she could have possibly dreamed the experience. She resolutely insisted that it had happened.

There had been reports by guests that they had seen figures moving about, and lights flashed on in their rooms, waking them from their sleep. Not much attention was paid to all this until I overheard Sarah Brown telling a group of summer camp riders about the two miners who come visit her when she is making up the beds and cleaning the rooms. I scolded her for this and said: "You'll frighten the children with your stories." She replied, "But Mrs. Coutu, it's true. When I turn the radio on they like the music, and they come to listen to the music and watch me making beds. They're both miners....They're rather tall and thin, and wear miner's caps with little lights in the front." Impossible! "Sarah, are you on anything? Drugs?" "No, no, I'm serious. It's happening."

I spent the next few days at the Dublin Library to research the history of the mine which had been on our property. I found that after the goldmine boom of 1850, mining became a prime occupation of many. In the late 1860s a group of Boston businessmen invested a total of $50,000 to set up mine operations and build a boarding house for the workers on this property. The boarding house was forty by sixty feet, exactly the dimensions of our lodge, excluding the decks. In walking our property, the only flat piece that could hold a building of that size, with necessary flat peripheral areas for moving horses and carts about, was exactly where we'd placed the lodge. The mining operations reaped very little in return for efforts made to produce. The boarding house was finally dismantled, moved to Keene, New Hampshire, and rebuilt as a livery stable. Could it be true? Were there possibly miners who had been injured in an accident, or simply died there at the boarding house, and were now coming back, bewildered, lost and forsaken, unable to find their lodging again?

*Growth and Riding Programs at Honey Lane*

✳ As time went on, we offered point-to-point trekking, with afternoon tea, dinner, and overnights in country inns along the way, exactly as we had experienced in riding in England and Ireland. The farm's byline was, *"A touch of Europe in the heart of New England."*

Within three to five years, sixty to eighty percent of each new group was comprised of returnees who took the first-time arrivals under their wings. We had so much fun and so many exciting events to relate. Evening at Honey Lane included storytelling of past adventures, singing, teasing, reviewing the day, and looking ahead to the following day's ride. Former FBI agent Dan Bledsoe, Master of Hounds of his foxhunting group in El Cajon, California, told us about his life as an FBI agent during the Watergate incident. Wow! We were intrigued by the "inside dope" that he shared with us. Mrs. Hattori, from Japan, with proper notice, and having had four hours of meditation in her bath, would dance for us. She was about eighty years old, tiny, with small black eyes in a face of porcelain skin. She would scrunch up her thin lips, strictly telling her audience that taking photos during her performance as absolutely not permitted until she was finished and was properly "posed," fan in hand, her exquisite kimono draping as it should, and those two little feet, clad in white socks separating the big toe from the others, were in their angled positions. When finished, she would graciously bow and thank her audience. Then she'd go to her room for a few beers! Yes!

Those guests who'd signed up earlier for a massage by therapeutic massage specialist Laurie Drogue, would each in turn, leave the group to enjoy the luxury of a good massage, concentrated on one's back, legs, and feet. Mrs. Shostakovich, daughter-in-law of composer Shostakovich, who had come to Honey Lane with her entourage of two children and a nanny, was disappointed when Al told her that the mushrooms she had gathered in a field in Connecticut, on the way to Honey Lane, would not be suitable for cooking as she'd asked, since he believed them to be poisonous. Despite my qualms, Mrs. Shostakovich proved to be an enthusiastic and friendly riding companion.

One of our riding guests with whom we've remained in contact was Christine Ebersole, who sang for us so beautifully, accompanied by Philip Buddington, an entertainer and master musician. Her beautiful voice and graceful presence transported us to another time, another place. We surely were spending the weekend in "Camelot." When she was not entertaining us, Christine would be rolling and playing on the carpeted floor in the lodge common room with our little granddaughter, Victoria. We still follow Christine's achievements with such pride. She has just opened in New York, starring in the new stage musical, *Gray Gardens*. Her stage reviews to date read as follows: "Christine Ebersole easily matches the achievements of Oscar winners Philip Seymour Hoffman (Capote) and Reese Witherspoon. Ms. Ebersole's performance is one of the most gorgeous ever to grace a musical." In 2002, Christine won the Tony award for best musical actress on Broadway. We consider ourselves privileged that God, or fate, brought her into our lives.

# Hay Rides with Mike, Jack, and Jill

✳ Jack and Jill, mother and son, were "paint" Percheron draft horses. They did not work hard or even daily, but needed care, feeding, grooming, and exercise every day. Our teenage "barn rats" and Mike Rich, the farm hand, would take turns jumping on Jack and Jill bareback, giving them a run. They were not built for speed but rather had shoulders, neck, and legs given to them by the Lord that were intended to do work. Heavy work.

The Honey Lane Lodge sat on the shoulder of Mount Monadnock. During the winter season, when sources of income needed to be created, we promoted a riding package, whereby an entire bank staff or commercial business staff would come for an evening to Honey Lane for dinner and a sleigh ride through our woodland paths.

Al prepared a dinner which reaped many compliments, and as always, served the meal in the large dining room, on the first level. The wagon held sixteen people, or eighteen or so if this was a "friendly" group, so guests alternated between having their ride and staying in the lodge. At the lodge, guests withdrew to the regal common room on the floor above the dining room. Warmth emanated from the wood fireplace, the game table was open, and the piano was played now and then. But guests mostly sat, chatting with the few riders who'd come from faraway places to spend a riding holiday, Thanksgiving, or Christmas with us. Outdoors, Jack and Jill, mostly the mother, Jill, trudged through crispy, dry snow. The bright moon above shone on the bundled-up wagon passengers and on the fallen snow, and the earth's cover reflected like diamonds.

One year, during the fall, we had been asked to host the New England Gem Association. They were to stay the weekend, overnight in the lodge, with meals provided by Al and staff. Dr. Rich, from Harvard, a specialist in the field of gemology, was to be the guest speaker on Saturday. After his lecture, he led the group up the path to the mine. Everyone brought hammers and small tools with them. I followed, and we all walked towards the mine area where Doctor Rich explained everything they saw. He could tell by the surroundings, the shafts, the holes, the slag, all that had happened there well over one hundred years ago. The twenty-five or so holes had been needed to provide light below ground where miners worked, as well as to hoist up the buckets and buckets of what could hopefully be gold. He pointed out the path which led from below to where we were up above. I realized for the first time that standing below to the other side of the path was a wall of immense width, an impressive sight, made of stone on stone, and progressively rising higher and higher from one end to the other. Up and down this path, work horses had drawn wagons carrying dirt, slag, logs, and wood for mine construction. There were many mounds of slag down below.

The guests hammered and picked away rocks of all sizes. Shining veins could be seen in many of them. Real or not? These chunks were transported back to the lodge in ladies' pulled-up skirts that formed a bag, or men's shirts. They resembled bulbous, deformed people. Several had thought to bring a bucket or container.

On that Sunday, a beautiful fall day, with vibrant, colorful leaves on tree branches everywhere, and a crunching of dried leaves underfoot, Michael began setting up the wagon for the horse-drawn wagon ride they'd requested. The wagon, quite a beauty, built of pine and oak, shellacked and finished with a luster not usually seen on farm wagons, could hold their entire group of sixteen people all at one time. The wagon had three walls, approximately four feet high. To the rear was only a yellow rope, attached from the end of one side wall to the other. Mike and Al loaded the hay bales and placed them like seats around the inside perimeter of the wagon.

A few days before, Al and I had taken our helper, Mike, by car, and laid out a map of which roads he would take the guests on. About one mile from the farm was a very, very steep hill which came past a large brick estate and then straightened out. On horseback, one either walks and leads his/her horse up that hill, or, with feet firmly in the stirrups, stands up and leans forward on the horse, so the rear pushing legs may "engage" and move ahead. Going downhill, a rider needs to be very careful, keeping complete control over their horse.

We told Mike to take them out in the wagon, reversing the path we would normally do on horseback, that is, going "up" the hill. By going in reverse, he would then arrive at the top of the hill, in front of the large brick estate, have his guests disembark from the wagon, pointing out the view of Mount Monadnock and a small ski area, suggesting that they take photos. Then they'd walk down the hill slowly and he would meet them there at the bottom. The wagon "brakes" could not have held the weight of sixteen people going downhill, but the horses holding back and the brakes, managed quite well with only Mike's weight.

While they were gone, I imagined the beautiful and memorable ride they would be taking, seeing rabbits, raccoons, the mountain range in the distance, open fields, many with cows, calves, and horses running alongside the wagon as it drove by. It was like "riding in a poster," one guest from England said. In England, she continued, "The leaves turn brown, and just hang there."

When I saw Mike and guests returning and driving up the rear path of our house, I, as usual, ran out, smiling, happy, with greetings for all, saying the customary, "How was your ride? Did you have a good time? Wasn't it fun?" The red-cheeked, now cold, city guests had no comments. Amazing! I looked at Mike and he grunted, and continued on ahead. *Oh my Lord, what had happened*, I wondered.

Well, I found out soon enough. Mike, apparently forgetting his instructions to take that ride in "reverse," had taken it upon himself to go just the opposite way. In recollecting, it may have been that Mike had gotten lost, saw where he was headed, and told himself he would make the best of the situation.

Well, with guests sitting on hay bales, on a highly glossed wood surface wagon, let the reader imagine every possible thing that happened as the horses and wagon started uphill. With nothing more than the yellow rope to the back, guests were sliding down bales of hay, and falling off the wagon into the road and/or onto the side gullies heaped high with fall leaves. One by one, grasping the yellow rope as a lifeline, they finally let go. Mike reached the top of the hill with not one passenger or hay bale in the wagon. Instead, angry jewelry store owners and gemologists were either looking through the leaves for their wallet, or their watch, or their glasses, etc., etc., and then, totally disheveled, disillusioned professional men and women climbed slowly up the hill. No one ever asked for their money back, but I bet we'd provided them with the absolutely best parlor story to tell that they'd ever personally experienced. That was a story that would last for a lifetime of retelling.

# Trekking

❋ Our usual four-day treks included being met in the woods by Al and me at lunchtime, and while some of the barn girls that we'd brought along with us watered the horses and brought them to a nearby brook or pond to cool their legs, lunch was served on a large portable picnic table. We tried to duplicate the style of European riding and included wine during the first days. However, people who had ridden for about four hours were tired and sweaty, and had a little difficulty with drinking the wine. After chatter with everyone comparing notes about the morning, either the rider could not remount, or would overmount and land on the other side of the horse. We scratched the wine from our lunchtime menu.

The afternoon would comprise riding to the first inn in which our horsemen would spend the night, arriving at about 4:30, the usual English tea-time. The inn hosts served scones and tea cakes, tea, and sherry after excited reviews of their afternoon, about whose horse took the lead; the deer they encountered; the small woodland animals; and the excitement of a hefty tree having fallen across their path, needing to be jumped, right in the midst of a rapid woodlands cantor. That was exciting. I can vouch for that, having been there myself. After tea, riders would then go to their rooms to shower and rest, and return downstairs for dinner at about 7:30 P.M. During each day, their luggage would be transported to the inn where they would spend their next overnight.

This was a project that had taken years to plan. Doing point-to-point trekking on horseback had required, first of all, exploring with all the little dotted lines on the light green geographic map, to find which of those old woodland trails, such as the King's Highway, the Old Dublin, the Old Antrim, and the Old Hancock and Harrisville dirt roads, were still open and passable. Through experimentation, and actually riding the trails, branch clippers in hand, we found during a period of three or four years, sometimes difficult but passable trails leading to thirteen or fourteen outlying villages. It was important that the treks would not have tar roads underfoot. Being miles inland, it was important that every detail of the trek would be taken care of in advance. It required staff meetings, details of each guide's responsibilities, and experience with resuscitation procedures. In the eighties, unlike today, no one used cell phones; however, the head trail guide had a portable phone, large and clumsy, attached to her saddle. It would bounce up and down, up and down, and slap against the horse's haunches every time the group had taken up a trot, canter, or gallop. Thud! Thud! Saddle pads with pockets contained items such as tape, sponges, water, and first-aid needs. On several occasions, through the years, injuries would happen to one horse or another from walking in deep beds of fallen leaves, not realizing until your horse's leg was trapped, that the leaves covered an old wire farm fence which long ago had collapsed and lain there underneath the colorful leaf camouflage.

With any luck, there might be a doctor in the riding group who could help retrieve a badly torn leg from the piercing metal and apply temporary first-aid, at least to help stop the bleeding, and hold until the next few miles when the woodlands had become little villages, where help could be sought. On some occasions, Pam would call a veterinarian on her phone from the accident site, tell the vet what happened and the location where the group would emerge from the woods, and the vet would be there waiting at the clearing to take care of his patient!

*Happenings at the Farm*

✳ For several years, Romy Roy, who ran an equestrian center in Haiti, would come in the summer with about sixteen or seventeen young riders. Hers was surely a facility for the very wealthy. These were the children and grandchildren of the Papa Doc era. Their parents and grandparents owned the docks, the sugar mills, the gas and electric companies, etc. They came for our daughter Lisa's training. Lisa would also be their coach for horse shows, and that was the prime reason for their being at Honey Lane. There were times that Romy would transport her young clientele to England or France for competition. They often went to Wellington, in Florida, to compete. Romy also would have liked Lisa to go to Haiti to give riding clinics, but granddaughter Victoria was very young, and we feared what could happen medically or otherwise.

These children were accustomed to having servants; someone to dress them, tie their shoelaces, and dry them off when they stepped out of the shower or bathtub. While Lisa taught them to groom and prepare their own horses, how to clean stalls, which they had never done, as well as work on their riding, the English instructors tried to teach them how to tie their own shoes, dress, and tend to their own selves.

Some of them were really little. They liked being waited on, but it wasn't going to happen at Honey Lane. They would run away and hide under furniture and little giggles could be heard here and there. The little boys were really cute, but little rascals. They also peed in the shower stalls. They were totally undisciplined, but ever so darling.

In the mornings, the children would come down to the spacious lodge dining room, and as the adults sat together, each child lined up, and in turn, gave a small "peck" on both cheeks of each adult.

Some parents came to visit from Haiti while their children were at the farm, and the same little "pecking routine" was followed by the parents as well. I especially liked when Uncle Fritz came to visit. I knew, from his telling Al, that he had a .38 caliber gun upstairs under his pillow, and that he kept this gun with him at all times for fear of being attacked, or being the victim in an attempted murder. His brother who'd run the mill with him in Haiti, had been duped by a group's ploy, and was murdered the year before. Dark and handsome Uncle Fritz made my trek to the lodge for breakfast well worth my while. I sure liked his cheek-to-cheek greetings.

During his trips, Uncle Fritz was also searching to purchase any abandoned sections of railroad track logs, wanting to rebuild tracks in Haiti as his own train conveyor system between his sugar mills and his cargo boats waiting in the port. I called riding friend Louise Mellon, whose family had railroad interests, asking if she knew if there were any sections of unused rail and ties which Fritz could purchase. None were available for sale. Apparently, the superannuated rails and logs had been negotiated for long ago.

*Adults*

✳ With the mix of riders who came to Honey Lane for a few days or longer, it was a done deal that each session would yield at least one good story. A few days ago, Lisa and I met with riding pals from New Hampshire at Wellington in West Palm Beach. We'd hoped to visit with old friend George Williams, who many, many years ago, rode at Honey Lane, and who is a nationally known dressage rider whose achievements in the show ring have been well documented. We missed seeing George, but had the pleasure of visiting with his sister, Jennie, and his brother, Stuart. Over lunch, we started reminiscing about some of the things that had happened at the farm.

Pam Godin talked about the day she and Lynne McEwan had taken Dr. Y, a Madison Avenue pediatrician, and his wife, on a backwoods trail ride to Hancock. On their return trip through the woods, a screeching of tires could be heard. Up ahead was a truck that had slipped off the muddy road, and the rear end had dropped into a gully. Out came the old gentleman, asking for help. While Mrs. Y, who was pregnant, stayed on her mount, Lynne and Dr. Y dismounted, handing their horse leads to Pam. Now Pam was on her own horse and holding two others. The old gentleman got back behind the wheel, and Lynne and Dr. Y began pushing in the rear. Mud was flying everywhere, the tires were spinning, making a sharp, groaning noise, and Willie, one of the horses Pam was holding, bolted. Pam was yanked out of her saddle and being dragged down the dirt road, over rocks and gravel, by two galloping horses, while still attempting to hold the reins to her own mount. The front of a completely new riding outfit was torn and ripped. Every bit of her body hurt and she had bruises and lumps that would hurt for days to come. Of course, I brought Pam to my shop, The Hunting Horn, and replaced her outfit, gratis.

After hearing the story, one of us said to Pam: "Wasn't Willie the leased horse who, when tied to a tree one day during a riding break, uprooted the tree, and ran back to the barn with the tree in tow?" Yes, it was, and uncontrollable laughter ensued.

In the meantime, back at the ranch on the same day, and approximately the same time as Pam's adventure, two English instructors, during "free time," wearing nothing more than three small bikini patches, came running to the house where Al was preparing the dinner meal. "Mr. Coutu, Mr. Coutu, Bailey fell on Heather." We ran out to the back sand exercise ring, and could not believe our eyes. There was Heather Castlehow, underneath the nearly seventeen hands Palomino Tennessee Walker. The horse had fainted during his riding instruction, and started to drop. Thinking that he would fall to the right, Heather prepared to dismount quickly from his left side. But the left side is exactly where he fell and just totally plopped over Heather! To the top of this setting, and coming out from under Bailey's back, was one of Heather's legs. On the forward side, under Bailey's stomach, Heather's head and one arm, were right in the middle of his two front legs and his two rear legs. We knew that, as soon as he started coming to, those legs would start to scramble and kick, and Heather would be badly hurt or killed. Al and Michael Rich, our farm hand, procured ropes as quickly as they could, tying one fore leg at the cannon, just above the hoof, and one rear leg also at the same place. They began rolling him up and away from Heather's head, and over to the other side. That procedure is also used when a horse is "caste," that is, he's rolled into a corner or wall in his stall, and cannot work his way out to stand up. Lisa said that if they hadn't been on the soft sand surface, that maneuver could have broken Bailey's back. Bailey revived and turned out to be fine. We think his collapse had been caused by the heat.

When the EMT's arrived, Heather was carefully placed on a stretcher. Coincidentally, one of the girls accompanying the medics, a novice volunteer, was also named Heather. When Jeff, the medic, would ask the patient, "Now, Heather, how do you feel?"

"Oh I feel great," the other Heather would say.

"Not you, Heather," Jeff would say, "this Heather, the one on the ground that we're taking care of." Then, when Heather, the patient, was asked if she could move her arms or her legs, the other Heather would do exactly that. "Not you, Heather. I'm talking to the Heather on the ground." The area was becoming crowded with police cars, another EMT vehicle, an ambulance, passersbys, curiosity-seeking drivers.

During all this commotion, Pam and Lynne's group arrived on the scene. They had been eager to tell us about the truck incident, to have us see Pam, scratched, wounded, and in tatters. But upon noticing that we were in our own muddle, they took the wisest and kindest course, leading their own horses into the barn, cooling them out, and settling them in their stalls. It was not until after dinner that their incident was revealed to all of us in the group. We all had a good laugh. It would always please me personally when reservations to ride at Honey Lane included "conditional to Mrs. C taking the ride out." After one of my more notorious treks, while our guests were getting into the van for our planned dinner at the Latacarta Restaurant in Peterborough, a doctor from Maine sat next to me on the passenger side and said, "If you drive like you ride, I'm buckling up!"

One morning in September, three riders wanted me to take them out as early as possible. There were predictions of heat into the mid-nineties by the afternoon. It was to be a very hot day. After grooming and tacking up our horses, we set out for the morning ride, Martha, Midge, Heather, and I. In lieu of riding down Goldmine Road and taking the sharp left onto gravel-covered Dooe Road, where we could pick up a nice uphill canter, we decided to cut through the narrow path behind the lodge, and walk carefully through a terrain of rock, slate, mounds of dirt and slag, and sinkholes from former goldmine operations. Nevertheless, it was truly an interesting ride. About a hundred years before, after gold had been discovered in the Black Hills of Dakota, the small mine hidden in the woods outside Dublin Village became of interest to investors. Five major businessmen came up with a total of $50,000 to set up mine operations there. To create access to the mine area, a father and son cut and cleared all trees for that half-mile fork away from Valley Road, and with oxen and rollers, created Goldmine Road where we eventually came to establish Honey Lane Farm.

We rode by one shaft which opened into the mine, and then hundreds of feet beyond another shaft filled with spring water, unlike the first which was dry but had debris of tree branches and other things. Eventually we passed through the small opening in the traditional New England stone wall which separated our property from our neighbors to the rear. Continuing on a narrow woodland path, up ahead on our left was a possible roadblock. A huge fir tree had fallen away from our path, but with its root system gone, up in the air, still attached to the tree's base, it had created a rather formidable hole filled with spring water. Did we dare try passing? There would be only about sixteen inches of path, wood and brush on our right, and an approximately five- by six-foot water hole to our left. I went on ahead, cautiously hugging the right side of the path, then Midge did the same, as well as Heather, one of our riding instructors from England. The fourth rider, Martha Schofield, from Darien, Connecticut, was several feet behind and still attempting to cross. From up front, I heard something that sounded like an "oops" and then a splash! Martha was in the hole, with water up to Stormy's shoulders. She too, like Pam before her, had just gotten new chaps and new shoes in my shop and all were drenched by muddy water. In struggling to move, Stormy slid left, coming to rest, leaning against Martha's left leg, her foot still in the stirrup, on the opposite side of the hole. Martha was trapped, and Stormy with one front leg, and both rear legs, tangled in the root system below, was hyperventilating. His right front leg continued to flail, desperately trying to release himself. I dismounted and tied my mare, Delight, to a tree up a little further. My initial try was to go to the other side, stand on the bank and take hold of the reins, and see if we couldn't move him up and then forward. I slipped off the muddy bank, and I too, was trapped, having twisted my right knee while sinking in, with mud and muck up to my knees, almost directly in front of Stormy's flailing free leg. With help from Heather, I eventually worked my way out and onto a drier portion of the bank, limping as I went to Martha and Stormy a few feet away. Martha is an experienced rider, a strong lady, calm as can be, though concerned about having to buy new riding breeches, chaps, and shoes, when she finally got out. Between customers like

Pam Godin and Martha Schofield, my shop, the Hunting Horn, was not working out to be a moneymaker!

Martha was stroking Stormy's head, speaking softly to him, quieting him down. Horses, when trapped like that, can very well die from fear and exhaustion. I'd sent Midge Gosling, a novice rider, on a new horse she had just purchased, to "hurry and get help." Midge and horse slowly found a path through the overgrown brush, continued into an open field on the Dooe Road side, passed through the wall opening, and walked down Dooe Road and up Goldmine Road. After awhile, she arrived at the farm, telling Al and Lisa (now very pregnant with Victoria), "Stormy's hoof is caught, and Aline needs a lead line." As Midge walked down Dooe Road, she'd told horse neighbors that we were having a problem. Quite a bit of time had elapsed between Martha's fall into the water and help coming. After Midge had left, Heather and I, each holding onto a young oak tree with one hand, prepared Martha for what we were going to do. On the count of "three," Heather and I would grab her with our free hands, and she was to grab our hands, so we could pull her up and out. I said, "If you can, bring the saddle with you." Martha unbuckled the cinch, and sure enough, on the count of three, up came Martha, holding the saddle with her right hand!

Every effort was being made to keep Stormy calm. A young, unseasoned horse would have died of fright and exhaustion in trying to free himself. Not Stormy. He was being stroked and told that all would be all right, help was on the way, and he had enough confidence from years of riding at Honey Lane that his masters would not fail him. At least one hour had passed from the onset of this event.

After a while, the first arrivals were the Stones, who lived on Dooe Road, then Gerry Christian, who delivered us barrels and barrels of water for the horses, on his truck, in the winter, when all our well pipes were frozen. Then Al and Lisa arrived with lead lines in hand. A few people had come to watch, and Gerry Christian was in the water hole with Stormy. Al shrieked, "Jesus Christ! Jesus Christ! What the Goddam is going on? You just don't need a leadline!" Gerry said, "Al, get in here with me"

"No! I'm cooking over there, I have people to feed."

"Al, this is your horse, take off your apron and get in here with me." Slowly, during the next thirty to sixty minutes, emergency crews were arriving, and someone drove a crane into that small woodland trail, covered and surrounded by fallen trees and a tangle of vines and branches, as the crane operator simply sat and waited. Betsy, a member of the emergency crew, a longtime friend and rider, called home to have her husband, Bob, bring some canvas stall guards down to the site. Bob did so, handed the stall guards to Al and Gerry in the hole, and went back to lean against the crane, talk with the crane operator, and watch the entire fiasco from his vantage point about twenty feet away. The area was surrounded with people, not even mentioning those who had simply come to watch. Gerry Christian and Al, both in the chest-deep water hole with Stormy, were placing the attached stall guards beneath and around Stormy's stomach. The heavy metal chain hanging from the crane was lowered and connected to the stall guards. Success! Stormy was slowly hoisted out, and four hoofs settled, a little shakily, on firm ground, and muddy or not, he was hugged by everyone who loved him and was kindly led out of the woods to the Stone farm, where he was washed, fed, and checked out by the veterinarian.

I was limping badly by now, and was asked by one of the medics if I wanted a ride back to the farm. As has always been traditional for me, I said, "No, thank you." I would make it on my own. Arriving home, I looked into the mirror and saw only two little holes with eyes peering back at me. I was totally covered in mud. Wearing my entire riding outfit, helmet, shirt, breeches, and boots, I climbed into the tub while the shower, at full strength, washed off most of the mud. Then, piling up my clothes, and putting them in a bag, I took a soaking bath to remove the mud on my body, in all the little corners. What an experience we'd all just gone through. I was proud of how our group of three, Martha, Heather, and myself, had handled that emergency—calmly, well organized, and without panic. It had been quite a day, but sadly, the day wasn't over yet.

While I was getting dressed to drive myself over to the hospital, Al returned, and he said, "You won't believe this! We'd all left the site, and as we were approaching the opening in the Dooe Road stone fence, Bob collapsed and died. "No!" I said in disbelief, but it was true! Bob had a weak heart, and had been working on his tractor in the 96-degree heat when Betsy called him to bring the stall guards. True, he'd made no rescue efforts after he'd handed Gerry the stall guards, but coming the distance from home, and walking over one quarter mile through shrubs and brush in the woods to the site had exacerbated his condition. But, as one doctor told me afterwards, "With Bob's heart condition and having worked on his tractor in that heat, he could have gone home, lifted a fork to begin eating, and would have died on the spot." Bob was a quiet, unassuming man who worked hard and had a weak heart. My thoughts went out to Betsy's family for losing a dad, especially since plenty of stall guards were in my barn and in my shop, close by, and they should really have been requisitioned from there, not from Bob, for whom this would be a strenuous request. I wondered why *I* hadn't thought of that, but there was simply too much going on.

I approached the hospital emergency entrance to have my knee looked at. A few people had gathered there, and Bob's daughter from a previous marriage ran to me. I tried to console her, but it was futile. I left the hospital with a leg brace which I was to wear for several weeks.

In the following days, the newspaper headlines read: "Man Gives Life to Save Horse." I was interviewed by TV, radio, and newspaper reporters requesting that I give them more and more details. Everyone was talking about brave Bob, who had sacrificed himself to save Stormy, the horse. Man-Gives-Life-to-Save-Horse Bob, whose life had been a simple one, with no outstanding achievements that I knew of, had died a hero! I endorsed the recognition and was very saddened that it had happened.

*My Life: "Mommy" and Pop*

✳ On rare occasions, my parents would make the trip from West Warwick, Rhode Island, to visit us in Dublin, New Hampshire. My mother was petite, and lived for earthly things, looking good, dressing well, and making a good impression. She'd spiff my father up with matching tie, belt, and breast-pocket handkerchief when they went out, and he appeared to be more like a city mayor and not the poor second cousin with the fourth-grade education she'd married years ago.

She would scrutinize our woodland lifestyle, not enjoying the experience, and say, "Well, if you like living like this" and walk away muttering I don't know what. On one or two occasions (I hope it was two!) I would harness up one of the horses to the horse carriage, and take my father riding on the woodland roads that were everywhere in Dublin. He was content sitting next to me, smoking his pipe. I'll always remember the scent of Copenhagen Blend when we were together. Here was a man totally at peace with the world, who'd had a difficult early life growing up in poverty in Shawanigan Falls, Canada. At age five, he'd contracted rickets due to poor nutrition. At age ten and eleven, he was working at the Shawanigan lumber mill, side by side with grown, rugged men, hauling in logs with heavy chains as they came down the river. My father's frozen fingers set into place, leaving some permanently crooked. Both my index fingers are crooked, not from arthritis or from getting old, but I was born that way. My father's gift, I think. When I look at those two crooked fingers now, my heart warms, as they are a reminder of a father whose love for me knew no bounds and who protected me as best he could. During my childhood, he was my friend, gave me encouragement, and kept my life sane.

We would never mention "Mommy" on the ride. At age twenty-six, handsome, athletic, and a former boxer, Arthur Ernest Forcier had taken his bride from a wealthy New Bedford family and brought her to live as the "barber's wife" in the mill village of Crompton, Rhode Island. Everyone knew my father "Jack" and they congregated at Jack's Barbershop, or across the street at Begos Café to play cards, which was an everyday activity. If you wanted a haircut, you just had to go across the street. Jack would be there with his usual stubby cigar in his mouth, playing cards. He almost always had a short, stubby cigar in his mouth. I wondered if they manufactured short, stubby cigars especially for my dad. I seldom saw him with a new, fresh cigar. In reflecting on the photos of my dad with his bowling buddies, his baseball team, shooting pool, or at a game of some sort, there was always the little cigar. I think now that those were happy times for him, and that he would not interrupt the moment to stop, throw away the stub, and open up a new one.

I never spoke to him about my childhood with my mother. I don't think he ever knew. I was an only child and when my dad was not at home, I had to deal with this formidable, demanding woman. My fear of her would not permit me to break any rules, but should I slip, various punishments were at hand. I would be tied, like a dog, to the large, round granite and chrome parlor stove which stood at the entrance of our living room. I would feel humiliated by anyone arriving and seeing me there, sitting on the floor, tied by my leg to the stove. Or, there were my father's leather straps, used to sharpen his razor, in back of the bathroom door. Those came in handy on occasion. I was twelve years old, and my mother was washing my ears. Yes! Believe it! She was reprimanding me for one thing or another, as usual, and I was trying to tell her I was a good kid. I even told her that, compared to *some* of the girls in my grade, she was *lucky* to have me. *They* were dating sailors from Quonset Point, and I certainly wasn't. She hit me so quickly, and so hard in the face with her hand, that I went reeling across the upstairs bedroom hall several feet. She was small but mighty strong, and I knew one thing! I would never mention the word "sailors" again.

Starting at the age of five, I walked every day the one mile, back and forth, from my house in Crompton to Christ the King School in Centerville. I never missed one day of school in eight years. As a matter of fact, when the big hurricane of 1938 arrived, almost totally unannounced, we children were all told to go home. I remember it well. I was age seven, running and skirting trees and electric wires which were coming down in back and in front of me. What a long mile that was.

Back then, classes began at 8:30 A.M. and ended at 4:00 P.M. I would leave home at about 7:00 A.M. to have my piano lesson, or practice before school started, and be back home about 4:30 P.M. My supper was nearly ready, I would do my homework, and even at age twelve, I was to be in bed at 6:30 P.M., before my father returned home from work for his dinner. Then, I would be out of the way. I could hear my dad arriving downstairs and would hope that he would come up to be with me a little. Usually he did, and usually he had an ice cream bar for me to eat while we chatted. After a few moments, he would say, "Mommy will be mad, if I don't go down now."

I was about nine years old when my parents and grandparents were driving to Canada to visit with relatives. We stopped at Old Orchard Beach in Maine. My dad and grandfather, Liboire Lapre (a J.D. Rockefeller lookalike, with a 17-inch neck, handsome and tall with silver hair, who walked with the stride of a man who knows he is very successful) went their own way, and my mother, my grandmother, and I went ours. I realized afterwards that I should have stayed with the guys. As we passed hot dog stands, sticky candy stands, etc., we came to the rides. One ride really interested me. I desperately wanted my mother and me to take the ride. It was the "Cave of Horrors." There were little wagons on rails being pulled by a small pony. These were all individual, not attached to a string of wagons or seats, but each going into the "Cave of Horrors" separately. "Let's do it, Mom...let's do it!"

My grandmother urged my mother to buy tickets and take the ride. My mother went to the ticket stand and returned. She had me climb into the little wagon, and I moved over to make room for her. She said, "Oh, I'm not going. You're the one who wanted this." I was petrified. I could see ahead of me a huge black hole, and the small horse was about to pull me in there. Even though my grandmother was telling her to get in with me, she absolutely refused. The pony started walking and at the first turn, my mother and grandmother disappeared behind me. I was in total darkness. Ghosts shot out of nowhere, huge subhuman beings came towards me, lurched at me, nearly touching me. My heart pounded and I screamed almost without stopping. Finally, it slowly became daylight ahead. I hadn't died or had a stroke. I was safe, after all. I dismounted from my box, heard my grandmother telling my mother what she'd done wasn't right. What on earth could she have been thinking? My mother looked at me and said, "At least, you won't be bothering me again." I didn't. Another "Mommy" lesson learned the hard way.

My father was my buddy. His buddies were my buddies. He was the fun part of my life. Big burly guys in my father's bowling league would patiently sit and wait while "Little Jack" (me) spun her three balls down the lane, usually into the gutter. I would go to the baseball games where he was pitcher for the mill team, the Velvet Villagers. As with his bowling, he could throw a curve ball that would drive the batter on plate absolutely crazy.

He would have had to be pulled away from the group of kids he'd entertain with tricks before the game started. "C'mon Jack, let's get going...play ball...play ball." To add to the irritation of everyone waiting for him to get started, he would stand at the pitcher's mound, do this large swing, ball in hand, go into the usual pitcher-at-the-mound contortions, bringing both hands to his back and then throw out the ball? Where was it? It had been passed to his other hand during his "performance," and nothing, absolutely nothing, was flying toward the batter. He was a constant tease and how he didn't get tarred and feathered was beyond me.

My mother arranged to have me go to a boarding high school, Jesus and Marie Academy in Woonsocket. I was happy there. Two nuns would wake us in the morning with violin music as they strolled the aisles between our small sleeping cubicles. My father had taught me to play baseball, throw some baskets, and skate (one year, he'd painted my old black skates white, so I would have white skates, like all my friends, for Christmas). I played just about every sport, and ran faster than anyone else.

There were no Interstate roads back then in 1945. My father would travel the one-hour drive to come see me play basketball.

Sometimes our team traveled to other schools and he would go there to see us. On rare occasions my mother would accompany him to hear me play at a piano recital. During my junior year, I'd become top piano student of the school. I would be selected to play for visiting dignitaries, the bishop, and other special events. At an important year-end recital, I remember my father being surrounded by students' parents who were doctors, lawyers, well-educated, well-to-do persons, as they praised him about how well I had "tackled the arpeggios," given a strong performance, and that he had "truly raised a child virtuoso." He sparkled, smiled, agreed with everything they said, and replied, "Thank you, thank you, thank you." He didn't know half of the words they used, but looked at me with such pleasure, such love, such satisfaction, calling me, as he always did when he was surprised and proud of any accomplishment I'd achieve, "My dumb cluck...my dumb cluck," all the time hugging me.

During the winter of 1947 and spring of 1948, while on my few weekends home, I began to notice that my father did not look well. He was losing weight and simply wasn't himself. His brother Larry, had had brain surgery in the fall, and my dad was the one on call to be there with him during seizures, keeping Larry's tongue away from his crunching and grinding teeth. Also, my mother's mother passed away on December 11, 1947, and my dad really loved her. My dad was a "softy." He loved too much, and the problems he was helping others cope with were bringing him down.

Recital time and graduation were approaching. My father said he wondered sometimes why he was cutting hair and was "not the person out on the wagon being pulled by a horse, calling out 'Rags...Rags'" as he went through our village. My dad's health matters were not going well. Old Doctor Mack said it was a cold. "Go home, rest, get some sleep...you'll feel better."

Two weeks later, I played last at the recital. I played Chopin's Valse Op. 64. It was all I wanted it to be for my dad. He would have been so proud. He wasn't there. I missed seeing the look of pride, the twinkling eyes, and the loving smile, and his calling me his "dumb cluck."

# Graduation

✳ The school was on a hillside. Two days later, we were all preparing for graduation on the lowest level of the school, exactly where part of the sidewalk outside slanted down and we could watch people's legs and feet coming down the hill toward the entrance to the school, where they would then go upstairs to the Grande Salle, the recital hall.

I watched and watched out that ten- by twelve-inch slanted window, looking to find my father's feet. More and more people went by, and I saw my mother's and her sisters' feet, but never saw my dad's. My heart sank. Jesus and Mary School gave two awards then at graduation, one for highest scholastic, and the other for highest piano achievement. That one was to be mine, and my father wouldn't be there. Even in writing this, I well up, remembering exactly my disappointment and broken heart.

After the ceremonies, we all returned home to West Warwick. Against the living room wall was the new Kohler and Campbell console piano my parents had purchased for me. Just beyond the piano sat my father, wrapped in a robe and blanket, seemingly unable to comprehend what was going on around him. My aunts said, "Aline, you must play something for us." I began playing "Liebestraum" by Franz Liszt. Within moments, I stopped. My father's face seemed to be turning to gray wax, and he was beginning to slump over from weakness.

Through many months ahead, my father recognized no one, not his mother, or his friends, or sometimes, even me. The big mustached smile was gone, and he would either cry or stare straight ahead. Any sound or smell affecting his senses would bring him to total collapse. There could be no smell of food cooking. When we spoke to him, we did it very slowly and very softly. He could not watch our lips while we spoke. Their movement would cause him to faint. Going away to a music school was now out of the question. I took a job, providing the only income, as my mother devotedly, and with unbelievable strength, took care of my dad. My heart and my fingers were longing to, but I did not touch the new piano for nearly one year. He could not tolerate noise of any kind.

My cousin Leo, the son of my mother's brother, Ernest, was to be married in New Bedford on May 30 of the following year. My father was beginning to be himself again, and he felt certain that he could drive the distance from West Warwick, Rhode Island to New Bedford, Massachusetts. On the return trip via Route 44 from Taunton, Massachusetts to Providence, Rhode Island, traffic was heavy on this narrow two-lane road. In Rehoboth about halfway between Taunton and Providence, a car up ahead was going very slowly. The first of two cars ahead of ours cut over into the oncoming lane, and the car exactly ahead of ours, did the same, getting ahead of the slow car. My dad started to follow, and was passing the slow car in the oncoming lane, but there'd been no room left for him to slide into. What happened next was so traumatic, so horrible, I remember it now with a heavy heart. We were hit by oncoming cars and were in the middle of a five-car pileup, front and behind. My mother's upper body lurched through the windshield, and much of her face remained on the windshield as she was thrown back into the car. People stopped to help. I was in the back seat. Two young men came and carried my mother over a slight swale on the side of the road, and placed her on the grass. It was May 30. Spring grass was growing, and little spring bugs, smelling the sticky, thick blood emanating from my mother's face and upper chest, were all over her. My father seemed to be beyond help. He was running up and down Route 44 crying and wailing. My mother's blood soaked even her corsets and flowed into the little swale, making a river everyone trying to help us walked through, and their shoes turned red. I know mine did.

It seemed to take forever for the ambulance to come from Taunton. Forty-five minutes, at least. I climbed into the ambulance with my mother, holding her hands while the attendant cleared her mouth so she could breathe, and tried to soak up the pools of blood over her eyes. As the ambulance was pulling away, my darling, dearest father, was running in the road after us. He was crying, calling, "Mommy...Mommy." I'd accepted the offer of two young men to take my dad to Hilltop, a club not too far away. They assured me they would take good care of him.

I held my mother's hand. I hoped that she would pass out, but she did not. I prayed softly, and tried to reassure her that things were not as bad as they seemed. I found out later that, inside her mouth, her jaw was broken, and her beautiful teeth, which she'd always prided herself on, were mostly broken. Her left cheek was a flap, opening right into her mouth. When we arrived at the hospital, the emergency room doctor, believing surely that she was unconscious, said, "Well, what have we here? Hamburger?"

I never knew the names of those two young men who kept my father with them, plying him with alcohol at Hilltop, and returning him to me at the hospital, at least having quieted him down. After a few hours, when my mother's surgery was over, and she was returned to a hospital room to rest, someone came to pick us up and drive us home.

My father was frail. The memory of what he'd done, and the guilt, was something we were living through every day. I worked in Mr. Soucy's office every morning, calling one of my parents' friends to drive us to Taunton in the afternoon.

I would scold my father on the way, telling him that he would not be permitted to stay in the room if he cried when he saw her. Our roles had changed. He was not the father I'd known. I'd become the parent, guiding and helping her child through this horrific time.

At night, when we returned from the hospital, I would sit on the side of his bed, stroking his head, talking and chatting with him until I finally bored him to sleep. After about a week or ten days of my being preoccupied with finding drivers with available cars, and hopefully keeping my father sane, Mr. Soucy fired me. I didn't blame him. I was so distracted and not doing my job justice.

Those two years had been tragic with my father's nervous breakdown, and the disappointment of his not being at my recital or graduation to receive the praise that would come, finally reaping the rewards of his working at the mill from 6:00 A.M. until 2:00 P.M. and then at his barber shop from 2:30 P.M. to 11:00 P.M., in order to provide for me an education well above our means. Then there was the accident, with my mother being disfigured, and my father's continuing feelings of guilt, when he would simply break down and cry. On occasion, when he eventually tried doing errands on his own, he couldn't remember where he'd left his car. The police would return him to our house, assuring Dad that he was "not to worry," they would "find his car and drive it home." Imagine I, who knew nothing, was in charge of a depressed, scarred mother, and a dad who would not, for a long time, be himself again.

Weeks and months passed and my mother had some plastic surgery done, but came to accept her face as it now was, and my father slowly, very slowly returned to cutting hair. Through the years, he joined bowling teams, played sports, started working out with his punching bag in the garage, and jumped rope, as we've all seen boxers do. He was beautiful, and he danced with such light feet, just as if he were still in the ring. When my children began coming, in the mid-fifties, they saw a great, happy "Pepere," and were always so eager to be with him. My father was in his late forties when all this happened. He died in 1976 at the age of seventy-four. Amazing, isn't it?

If my mother was not unbalanced before her accident, she certainly showed many signs afterwards, especially after my father, whom she'd been so devoted to, passed away. She would relate to me that she'd thought her "arm was broken" and carried it bent, against her body. Then at some point, the doctor told her, "Mrs. Forcier, there is nothing wrong with your arm. It isn't broken." She was so pleased to hear that news, she showed me, moving her arm in every direction. "Wasn't that wonderful?" she said.

The day after my father's burial, I drove her to her attorney. While in the waiting room, I heard her screaming uncontrollably, at the highest pitch possible. I ran in to ask what was wrong. My mother was yelping and screaming, saying, "It's mine, it's mine, not hers, she never worked for that, I worked for that." The attorney said that a portion of my father's property was to come to me, and that's what my mother was so distressed about. I thought she would have a stroke.

I said, "So, what do we do?"

He said, "I can prepare a codicil, and you can sign off," which I did.

Al said afterwards that releasing between fifty and seventy-five thousand dollars was a big decision affecting all our family, the children's education, etc., and that I should have discussed this with him. But I couldn't. She was hyperventilating, red as a beet, and I thought something would "blow" and she would die right there. I said, "Look Al, in a few years, me being an only child, we'll get the whole thing anyway." Right! At my father's wake, she strode over to me, drawing quite a bit of attention to herself by coming over to me and handing me a white envelope. Later, an aunt asked about it. "I saw your mother giving you an envelope, money I presume?" I smiled and showed her the contents of the envelope: my father's driver's license and his bus pass.

We tried to keep my mother occupied during the next months, picking her up in West Warwick and driving her to the farm to be with us. We sometimes would bring her to the bus station in Keene for her return trip home. Letters to me began coming, cursing, rambling on and on, and when enough were stuffed into any envelope, they would be mailed, with no signature, no greeting, and then another stuffed envelope would come telling me that my father never could stand me, that I wasn't loved by him, and that I was in the way.

"It's so sad, Aline that your mother never loved you," one of my father's sisters told me. But then another sister said, "But it wasn't her fault, Emelia, she never wanted her." I'd always known that there was no warmth, no hugs, no praises to me about my achievements, except when she would put on her "show" boasting about what I'd done, and also many things I didn't do. (She told her friends I was in television when I was actually selling TVs in a retail store). When my mother passed away in 1993, her will read, "To my daughter Elaine (sic) I leave nothing. She has everything she wants." Meaning presumably that I had Al, and had married him after she'd said "Go ahead...get married!...It'll never last!"

*Riding and Shopping Abroad*

✳ On a weekend in October, we'd been asked by a freelance writer if we would host a visit by members of the Irish Horse Board. The woman, whose name I've forgotten, said they would not stay long, but Honey Lane had been suggested to them by the editors of the *Horsemen's Peddlar* as an example of resort riding we were doing in New England. She said they wouldn't stay long, but they would like a tour of the farm and the opportunity to speak with some of our riding guests. Seven men arrived. Six were Irish, and one gentleman was English. Some were bearded and all wore tweed caps. They had riding barns and lodging very similar to ours in Ireland, and were actually looking to recruit potential clients for their own riding stables in Ireland. They stayed through dinner, showing slides of their horses and housing facilities, explaining what riding levels were needed to join one of their groups. At about 11:00 P.M., Al and I bid them "goodnight, and thank you for coming," returning home to go to bed. I have no idea at what time the mutual admiration society broke up at the lodge dining room.

The next morning while having an exhilarating canter on the dirt roads around Dublin Lake, one rider to the rear of the four in tow, called up to the front, "So, when are we going?"

I shouted back, "Going where?"

"Going to Ireland to ride," she answered.

"Never!" I replied.

Not so! Too many wanted to go riding in Ireland. I made arrangements for flights, transportation, overnights, including with

Tilman Anhold, of Horse Holiday Farm in Sligo, County Donegal, one of the several members of the Irish Board whom we'd hosted. In addition to Al and I receiving a riding discount from Tilman, I also received travel agent discounts, which included one free fare on Aer Lingus for every fifteen people in our group.

Our early Friday evening departures from Boston had us arriving at Shannon Airport at approximately 8:00 in the morning. I'd planned every phase of our trip very carefully and well ahead. We were "collected" by a coach with large windows, and delivered to Mary Brown, whose Bed and Breakfast was just a short distance from the airport. After the first year, Mrs. Brown, who knew of our early scheduled arrivals, would withhold the number of rooms we needed from Friday evening availability, showing us our accommodations in the morning, as we arrived, then serving us an Irish breakfast of meats, eggs, potatoes, and "bangers."

While we spent our weekend in Shannon as tourists, we took in as much of County Clare as we could. Ireland is knee-deep in charm. Although this largely rural nation has transformed itself over the past couple of decades into one of Europe's biggest economic successes, I'm told it hasn't lost its friendly ways or its links with its traditional culture. We enjoyed the tour of Bunratty Castle and the usual toast of mead. The medieval banquet and Old Irish entertainment were a delight with the actors and singers dressed in elegant medieval costumes. Of course, there would be the king and queen, seated on their thrones. The musicians and singers, dressed in long velvet gowns of the period, were beautiful and superb, well above our expectations.

Traditionally, as in the mid-1500s, we ate with one utensil only—a small knife, not much larger than a pocket knife. Another evening, the well-known pub "Durty Nellie's," where entire families and children of all ages gathered, was truly quite a remarkable happening. Everyone joins in the singing and drinking, of course!

We found when we boarded the coach and moved on to Horse Holiday Farm in Sligo the next day, that now, well away from the oft-trodden tourist areas, the charm hadn't ended. At Horse Holiday Farm, each morning after breakfast we rode on horseback, cantering and galloping through open fields, then walked or trotted through town after town filled with brightly painted buildings and small shops, not very far from the ocean which slapped up against the cliffs beneath us, as we rode along the summit ridges. I have photos showing my horse's ears in the lower portion, with the wind so strong that it flattened out the long grasses before us. On the first day, we found it a little tricky to get to the beach and the dunes, which we could see from the breakfast room window. There was no direct path to get to the beach, approximately 300 feet in distance. Separating the Anholds' property from the next-door neighbor's were stone pilings, stones of all sizes which needed to be maneuvered, and this five-foot-wide path was our only access down to the beach. After the first time, we totally trusted our new mounts to step very carefully, and walk their way on the slightly sloping path. Tilman and those immediately behind him were the first arrivals at the beach, and each waited for the last riders to arrive. Ahh, at last, we were all on firm beach soil.

Totally unexpectedly Tilman shouted, "Let's go!," pointing forward, and taking up an immediate gallop. Twenty people, some experienced riders and some novice riders, were going in every direction, willy-nilly. I, holding on for dear life to the pommel of the saddle, was trying to do the impossible by having my horse, Bilko, slow up a little. No use. Coming up from the rear, cutting a swath through the other riders, and galloping the fastest pace of anyone, came Al, riding Lightning, the craziest terror horse that Tilman owned! Seeing Al surpassing the entire group, I gasped, knowing this would not have a good outcome. My nearest riding companion shouted, "Wow! I didn't know Al could ride." I shouted back, "He can't!" Al said later, he thought his life would come to an end!

Arriving at a gallop at the dunes, riders fell from horses that were shoulder-high in sand. I took Tilman aside and said, "We don't ride like the Irish. We're not cowboys."

Tilman responded, "I know, but I like to get it out of everyone's system right on the first day out. Otherwise, I keep being asked, "'When are we going to run?'" The following days were easier, and we were advised, in advance, what to expect.

During our rides through quaint Irish villages, it was always very easy to find someone to hold the horses while we stopped at a village pub to " 'ave a pint." We found the pace of the Irish people to be extremely relaxed. They were very friendly, with farmers giving us a smiling "thumbs up" as we passed, and people taking time off for an amiable chat.

Evenings were spent in pubs, meeting Irish countrymen, singing, drinking of course, and listening to the Barleycorns. What a group! I regret not having purchased one of their CD's. We'd return, exhausted, at about 2:00 A.M. Ireland usually always has morning fog, so breakfast would take place between 9:30 and 10:00 A.M. the next day.

We led several riding trips to Ireland, where after galloping beaches and dunes and enjoying the hospitality of our German/Irish hosts, we would drive north into Donegal Bay, and visit with crofters in the small fishing villages along the north coast of the bay, stopping to place orders with manufacturers of woolens and leather goods. For the flight back to New Hampshire, each rider had their $400 customs limit of *my* purchases in their luggage. Arriving home, we had riding goods (tack), saddlery, carriage robes, and woolen sweaters and jackets that would be featured in the Hunting Horn Catalog. For those riders not residing close enough to come to my shop to buy before coming on their planned riding holiday to Honey Lane Farm, these items would be shipped or would be at the farm, awaiting their arrival.

Al and I, just the two of us, made several trips to Ireland. We drove to and stayed overnight at the scenic bay of Dingle, and drove around the Ring of Kerry, continuing on into Waterford not only to see the glassworks, but also to order sheepskin, the sheep going directly to the slaughterhouse where they were killed, processed, and skins cured. We made arrangements with the owner, totally bloodied from head to foot, of how many sheepskins he was to ship. These would be used at the farm and sold in my shop as saddle pads. These plushy skins, approximately two and a half by three feet, were also used as chair throws or on the floor, by one's bed. We continued north along the eastern coast, going into Dublin, kissing the Blarney Stone, and stopping at the Avoca Mills to order woolen goods, sweaters, and blankets.

Several buying trips were taken to England. Driving out of Heathrow Airport was a lot more confusing and difficult than flying in. Circling around and around to uncertain exits, trying to get out of our lane, was not easy. We'd experienced the same confusion and fear while in one of the eight lanes circling around the Arc de Triomphe in Paris. We prided ourselves on being seasoned travelers, but there are certain instances that I would prefer not to relive!

In London, we stepped out of the elevator and found the smell of leather intriguing as always. On the fourth floor of Lillywhite's, at Piccadilly Circus, we were surrounded with horse goodies of all kinds. My contact in London, Elaine B., was one of the directors in her company. She personally managed this retail outlet at Lillywhite's, but she was also the purchasing agent for the company's sixteen other retail stores. Through her, we could order saddles, bridles, leather goods, horse wear, and Barbour jackets, at five percent above her cost, making my store back in New Hampshire, and my prices, very competitive. We walked on Bayswater Road, along the stone walls and gates of Hyde Park, for a distance of easily one mile, where, on Sundays, paintings, brasses, and a miscellany of goods were on display for sale. We shopped at Portobello Road, at the stalls at Covent Garden, where everything imaginable is available for purchase, always bringing back with us the unusual at very good prices.

We enjoyed our stays in England, touring much of the island, staying in Bath, Plymouth, Oxford, Bournemouth, and the Yorkshires, and visiting Stonehenge nearby, while overnighting at the Salisbury Inn with its time-worn sloping floors and circa-1500 architecture on Old New Street.

Much of London was appealing, and we stayed for a few days in a Bed and Breakfast, which had been in the late 1800's and until the turn of the century, the sometimes love nest of Lillie Langtry and Bertey, Prince of Wales and later Edward the Seventh. The home had now been converted into a boarding house, with mid-Asiatic cuisine permeating throughout each level.

While touring the Tower of London and visiting the sixteenth-century Chapel of St. Peter inside the Tower's walls, it felt strange walking on large, uneven flat stones, knowing that underneath, bodies of those executed on the Tower Green and Tower Hill in the 1500s and 1600s had been buried. Two of Henry the Eighth's wives, Anne Boleyn and her cousin Katherine Howard, among other notables, are buried in their coffins under the marble slabs in front of the altar in the chancel. As novices, we found the English restaurant fare different, the homes and small front gardens interesting, and the people themselves charming and helpful. We managed to see two musical stage plays during our several trips, *42nd Street* and *Evita*.

# *Run! Run Faster!*

✳ The traffic on the Via Veneto in Rome is almost beyond
description. My quest to find quality Italian gloves, suitable
for riding, had proven unsuccessful. Taxis were driving abreast of
three or four other speeding vehicles, sometimes so close to people
waiting to cross on the sidewalk that one wonders why there were not
bodies everywhere. Al and I were waiting at the crosswalk on Via
Veneto, and a speeding taxi passed us so fast and so close, that Al
actually kicked the taxi as it passed. The driver came to a screeching
halt. The door opened, and a man of formidable size stepped out. He
started running towards us. Al grabbed my hand and said, "Run!
Run!" Looking behind him and seeing our impending doom, Al said,
"Run faster! Run faster!" The driver had left his taxi in the middle of
this busy thruway. The green light was on, and horns were beeping,
Italian taxi drivers swearing, "Move, move!" They were screaming
and our assailant was forced to stop chasing us and return to his taxi
and drive on. We had been saved by Italian taxi drivers! With all our
travels abroad, after having visited Rome, receiving Pope Paul's blessing from his apartment balcony, walking the ruins of Pompeii, and
purchasing exquisite marble items from a small shop in Napoli, I was
never again tempted to revisit Italy.

*Goodby, Dearest Friend*

 *"And when the earth shall claim your limbs, then shall you truly dance."*

At the funeral, Maria Day Hyde sang an emotional "Amazing Grace." I sat, listening, and wondered, *Why are we here? Why is my husband who was so healthy, so strong, so active, no longer here with me, but in that small black box on the altar? What happened? What happened? Why am I looking ahead to a life without the person who is so close to my heart, to whom I said every day, "I love you so much. You've made my life so happy."*

When we left Jack's condo at Narragansett, on Labor Day 2005, we flew to Phoenix to spend a few days in Arizona and see the Grand Canyon for the first time. Lisa had said, "Go somewhere, but don't come back here to Florida. It's hot, it's humid, and buggy. Take a trip." So, after seeing Dr. Laura in Wakefield, Rhode Island, who'd been following Al's irregular blood pressure readings and had given him a new medication to try while we were traveling, we flew into Phoenix, then drove directly to Flagstaff. During the next days we visited the Grand Canyon and watched our Florida team, the Dolphins, win the football game on television while we sat at the bar of the Canyon Breeze in Sedona, with a few new friends.

The following Thursday, September 15, we flew back to Rhode Island. On Friday, September 16, we checked in on the young University of Rhode Island student who had leased Jack's condo for the school year, and visited with Dr. Laura. Al's blood pressure read

120/80. "Al," she said, "there's absolutely no reason why you shouldn't start driving back home to Florida."

The next morning, after driving two or three miles, Al stopped over at the side of the road. He said he was having trouble focusing, so I took over the driving. Arriving in Darien, Connecticut, I pulled in to the McDonald's and thought that having a Coke would give each of us the caffeine we needed. Returning to the car, I sat on the passenger side with my Mapquest map on my lap. I would need to follow directions through New York, so Al would need to take his turn in driving.

I settled myself in, put the vibrating pad on the seat against my lower back, buckled up, and said, "Okay, I'm ready, let's go." Then, silence. I repeated that we "should get going."

Haltingly, Al said, "I can't."

"What do you mean?" I replied.

He said, "I can't drive."

Kidding as always, I said, "*I know that*, I've been telling you that for years."

Al said, "I'm serious, Aline, I can't move my left arm and there's a lot of pressure on my chest." I unbuckled, ran around the car to his side, put my ear against his chest, listening to his fast, irregular heartbeat, then ran into the McDonald's to call 911. Within five minutes, help had arrived, an oxygen mask was placed on his face, and his mouth was sprayed with nitroglycerine. He was brought into the EMT wagon, and remained there for a long time, while being stabilized. A doctor pulled up next to the EMT vehicle and went in.

I was told later that when asked if he'd had a history of heart problems, he said, "No."

"But then, Mr. Coutu, what do you think brought on this heart attack?"

Al replied, "My wife was driving." Touché! Even in his condition, he was quick-witted in "returning the ball to my court"!

He was transported to the Stamford Hospital, where hours were spent trying to determine exactly what had happened to him. Could it be a thyroid condition gone wrong? Could it be this or that? It had truly been a heart attack! This was Saturday, and tests would be taken on Monday morning. Being told that I would not leave, that I had nowhere to go, the nursing director found a room for me quite near Al's.

On Monday morning, Dr. Portnay came out of the examination room. Al's condition "was serious." He needed a triple bypass, and named another problem as well. He was to be transferred to St. Vincent's Hospital "immediately." The ambulance left for Bridgeport at high speed. I followed, and after taking two wrong turns, finally arrived at St. Vincent's. I found him in CCU, Continuing Care, where by now he was hooked up to oxygen and intravenous tubes. I had not been too happy that the night before his departure from the Stamford Hospital, I'd arrived in his room and a nurse was carefully explaining to him the procedures that are required for open-heart surgery. She told him that the breast bones would be broken open, there would be incisions in his leg to remove usable veins, and she related to him what the success results had been in the past. He didn't need to know all that. Al had not been in a hospital for over forty-five years, when he'd had his tonsils out. Also, his surgery was not scheduled until Wednesday afternoon! Two more days! Although he would not show it, he was totally in fear.

One nurse arrived and said she'd found a room for me at the Ramada Inn nearby. A social worker arrived and said, "There's a lady up the street who rents out rooms and she has one for you."

I said, "I'm not leaving."

"But you can't stay here," they replied. "We have no rooms for you, and hospital policy is that family may stay nearby but not in the hospital."

I said, "You do have a pillow, don't you?" If they thought for one moment that, after fifty-six years of being with Al, through thick and through thin, that I would even consider leaving his side, especially at a time when he needed reassurance, they were wrong. I wasn't going anywhere.

About ten minutes later, a nurse walked in and gave me the good news that they had "found a room" for me. Wonderful! Thank you! The room was about eighty feet away from Al's. His room was about fifteen feet from the "visitor's corridor," take a left, and my room was approximately fifty feet down the hall, on the right-hand side. Lisa had flown up from Florida. Mike and his family from New Hampshire came to visit, as did friends from Providence, Rhode Island. Al had been stabilized and felt rather comfortable, and he had hospital staff coming in to see how he was, especially Sister Rachelle, who spoke French with him. So it wasn't all bad.

I spent most of my days with him...getting into his bed first thing in the morning. He would move over when he was aware I was in the room, and would pat the space next to him. We hugged, told each other how much we loved each other, and talked about what we would do, which plays we would go to, when we returned to Florida.

On Wednesday afternoon, he went into surgery, and was placed in the Intensive Care Unit afterwards, with all the usual attachments to his body, blood pressure equipment, an electrocardiogram, multiple intravenous and chest tubes, a respirator, plus the breathing tubes in his mouth. The tubes stayed in a for long time, as each time the nurses tried removing them so he would breathe on his own, his blood pressure would go up.

After he was returned to his room in the CCU, he still had several connections, as listed above. I would be up during the night, as I had been right along, and would go to his room to be certain he was sleeping and comfortable. After his return to the CCU, we worked my way around the tubes and I would get into his bed and snuggle and hold him.

I believe it was Friday that his brown teddy bear was gone. I said, "Al, where is your teddy bear?"

He had a guilty look. Al had a lot of difficulty speaking, as the tubes had made his throat and breathing very labored. He said, gasping, "The male nurse is really upset with me...(gasp) I'm in a lot of trouble (gasp)."

He looked so cute, and giggling, I asked, " So...what happened?" Again, speaking with difficulty, he explained that no one had answered his buzzer, that he really needed to pee, and had tried getting to his toilet, dragging all his paraphernalia with him. He'd dropped the teddy bear, and had peed on him. He felt terrible. He said he was told he couldn't have another one. (The teddy bears are used to press against the chest when the patient needs to cough.) I was there now, and it wasn't too long before Al had another teddy bear...a gray one this time.

On Saturday morning, he was now disengaged from his lifelines and the nurse was preparing him for his walk. I asked if I could walk with him. I asked Al, "Would you like to see where I live?" Hand in hand, with his Johnny open in the back, but wearing jockey shorts, we walked out of his unit, turned left, and about fifty feet down the corridor, I showed him my room.

He said, simply amazed, "You live *here?*"

"Yes," I said, "come in and see how nice it is," especially since Mike had gotten the head of maintenance and two of his crew to go into the room and make some changes. Originally, the room had one couch, light coverings, one chair, and one small table. The plasma TV was so high up near the ceiling that I would have to jump up, holding my shoe by the toe, and hit the side of the TV with the heel of my shoe. There would be one channel only, either "On" or "Off." The lights were sensor-controlled, so a blinking or slight movement had the lights on all night.

Now, Al saw a room with two chairs, the table, sensors disconnected, blankets on the bed, a TV remote control, and my laptop working and online, thanks to Mike having charmed one of the girls in the office to come up and get me hooked up.

We were always hand in hand, or I was in bed with him. Visiting hours meant nothing. We were the senior citizen Romeo and Juliet, and all the staff smiled when they saw us together. After checking on Al, as I always did during the night, I overslept until 7:30 A.M. on Sunday morning. I dressed hurriedly and went to his room. "Oh, Al, I'm so sorry I'm late."

He smiled. He said, gasping for breath, as usual, "Do you know what I did this morning?"

"No, what did you do?"

"I got permission...(gasp)...I got permission."

I said, "Permission for what?"

"I got permission from the nurses (gasp) to go visit you. They were laughing," he said, "I don't know why?"

*I can well imagine, seeing Al going off and into the visitors' corridor, with the back of his Johnny open, and very possibly, no jockey shorts on.* "So," I said, "I was there, what did you do?"

He said, "Your door was locked."

"Al...why didn't you knock?"

"I know you don't sleep much, coming in during the night to see how I am (gasp), and I didn't want to wake you." *Tears roll down my face as I retell this incident, feeling so deeply the inconceivable undying love we had for one another, and the hugs I would have had that will never be replaced.*

Sunday evening, we were snuggled together watching the Patriots game when Dr. Portnay came in. I thought all the doctors had gone home, was a little embarrassed, but lay very still, motionless, hoping I was invisible next to Al, while the doctor did his checkup, and asked him questions. "So, are you eating? You've got to keep up your strength."

I couldn't stand it. I quickly sat up, saying, "No! He isn't eating, he isn't eating. Look at his tray...nothing's gone."

Doctor Portnay looked at the tray, and slowly turned back towards us, saying, "Albert, you've got to eat your dinner, or you won't get lucky tonight." He smiled at us "golden agers," behaving as if we were teenagers falling in love.

Although Drs. Rose and Squiterri, the surgeons, both recommended that Al spend "two weeks upstairs in rehab," we were told by office clerks that we would have to leave the hospital six days after surgery, as Medicare would not accept any charges after that time. Lisa and I looked around for a safe place to stay. We found it at the Marriott Residence Inn in Milford, Connecticut, and reserved a room for two weeks. When we arrived with Al the next day, he looked around, and said, "Can we afford this?" just as he had asked many years ago while we were eating at a small café in the south of France.

I replied, as I had back then, "Of course not."

"Oh...okay," he said.

Lisa returned to Florida to tend to her equestrian business, but my cousin Jackie Garland came to the hospital and helped us move into our suite at the Marriott. She grocery-shopped and got us settled for what was to be a two-week stay.

The visiting nurse seemed to enjoy her visits with us, and always gave Al a good report. We walked as Al was instructed to, and drove to Bridgewater for Al's final checkup with surgeon Dr. Squiterri. On sunny days, we would walk a little, then climb into our convertible, putting the roof down, and play our *Chicago* CD as loudly as we felt anyone could stand it, while we kept the beat going with our hands against the outside of the doors. Hotel clients going in or coming out would smile at us, surely wondering if we'd gone into a second childhood.

At night, I would pull up my pajama top, and his shirt, and put my body against his chest, hold him close, thinking that in some way, I was sharing his surgery and his pain.

Then, it happened...that day at the Marriott, October 8. Al awoke and said, "I feel so happy." That was such an unusual thing for Al to say.

"Why are you happy?" I replied.

"I feel so good, nothing hurts."

And I said, "You've never complained about pain."

"I know," he said. "But this is different, as if I am whole, with no surgery on my body."

"Well then," I said, "would you like to get dressed and walk with me to the dining room for breakfast?"

"Nope! It's so nice here, I don't want to leave this feeling I have."

About twelve or fourteen minutes later, I returned to the room with breakfast on a tray. Not seeing Al in bed, I called out to him, and he answered from the bathroom. He came out, looked at the tray on the table, and said, "I feel dizzy right now, I'll lie here on the couch for a little while, then have breakfast." I didn't realize, but the countdown on the minutes of life he had left had begun. About thirty or forty seconds later, I asked him if he was still dizzy. He said, "Yes." Then about thirty seconds later, I asked him again if he was still dizzy. "Yes," he replied. Then the third time when I asked if he was still dizzy, he said, "No, but I can't breathe." Two shallow breaths followed. He gasped, and then he died, just like that. He died of a massive pulmonary embolism. A blood clot. My God, my God! The love of my life was gone! My nightmare had begun.

So now...here we are at Al's funeral, with friends from everywhere who have come to share our family's grief. I pondered while sitting there if Al, that Saturday morning, had a premonition that he was going on to his life's reward. Had he seen Jack? Was Jack with him during those last minutes? Jack who was always so brave, so courageous, and so funny. *Could be*, I thought.

The Lord's Prayer is being said. Then closing sentences, the Benediction, and dismissal are being spoken by Reverend Susan.

Reverend Victoria Burdick had wondered in her opening statements, when the funeral began, whether the Pearly Gates would open for Al. Exactly at 1:00 P.M., when Nancy began playing the postlude and the congregation was exiting the pews and walking down the stairs from the church, the rain and gloom that had prevailed through the week since Al's passing, suddenly stopped! The clouds disappeared and the sun shone brightly! THE PEARLY GATES WERE OPEN! And Al was surely with his beloved son.

We all smiled and chuckled, and several people looked to the sky and applauded.

Goodbye, dearest friend. I will always love you.

Albert lives on and on...

March 21, 2006

Mrs. Aline Coutu
741 Pirate's Rest Road
N. Fort Myers, FL 33917

Dear Mrs. Coutu,

One behalf of the New England Organ Bank and myself, I extend to you and your family my sympathy on the death of your husband, Albert. I am writing to you today to inform you of the status of Albert's tissues. I hope this information is helpful, and offers you and your family some sense of closure for your generous donation. Your ability to think of others during such a difficult time is both admirable and inspirational.

We were able to recover Albert's orthopedic tissues, which are used to hasten recovery in individuals suffering from bone or spine disease or injuries. The donation records indicate the creation of eighteen bone grafts, which have been, and will continue to be distributed to medical facilities throughout the country.

Donated skin is primarily used for the treatment of burns. Skin is also used for cleft lip repair, cancer reconstructive repair, and certain dental procedures. A small percentage of skin grafts are used in doctor's office-based procedures. So far thirty-five skin grafts have been produced from Albert's skin donation.

We do not yet have all of the implant information, but clearly Albert's gift will surely play a major role in the lives of others, and their families. Your decision to donate is itself a wonderful gift and tribute to your loved one. If you have any further questions, please do not hesitate to contact me. Our thoughts and support remain with you.

Warmest regards,


Kelley J. Green
Aftercare Coordinator
Donor Family Services


"*Al Lives on and on . . . . . .*"